Know Your Numbers

Circle or write the correct answers.

1. Which number is forty-one thousand five hundred thirty-six?

    a. 41,563   b. 401,536   c. 41,036   d. 41,536

2. Write the word form of the numerals.

   1,683 _____

  21,379 _____

3. Write the expanded form of the numerals.

    749 _____

  9,681 _____

    309 _____

  7,439 _____

4. Read the expanded form, then write the standard form of the numeral.

  800 + 60 + 7 _____

  4,000 + 200 + 70 + 3 _____

  400 + 60 + 7 _____

5. Circle the thousands place in the numerals.

    3,489   79,473   19,341   473,618

6. Circle the ten thousands place in the numerals.

    475,614   1,649,541   817,683   5,649,196

7. Circle the hundreds place in the numerals.

    1,443,623   16,945   7,485   516,689

Show What You Know

1. Round the following numerals to the nearest ten.

    43 _____   17 _____   61 _____   85 _____

2. Round the following addition and subtraction sentences to the nearest ten, then perform the operation.

    46   38   22   51   87
    + 18 + ___ + 27 + ___ + 73 + ___ + 12 + ___   + 69 + ___

    74   57   92   39   64
    − 48 − ___ − 29 − ___ − 43 − ___ − 9 − ___   − 38 − ___

3. Write the addition and subtraction fact families for each set.
    (7, 12, 5) _____
    (14, 8, 6) _____
    (8, 7, 15) _____
    (9, 4, 13) _____
    (16, 8, 8) _____
    (9, 17, 8) _____

4. Write the multiplication and division fact families for each set.
    (7, 6, 42) _____
    (32, 8, 4) _____
    (7, 8, 56) _____
    (9, 4, 36) _____
    (3, 8, 24) _____
    (5, 4, 20) _____

5. Write the inverse operation for each number sentence.
    6 x 5 = 30 _____   7 x 3 = 21 _____   8 ÷ 2 = 4 _____   18 ÷ 9 = 2 _____
    56 ÷ 8 = 7 _____   6 x 9 = 54 _____   36 ÷ 6 = 6 _____   6 x 4 = 24 _____
    9 + 4 = 13 _____   5 + 6 = 11 _____   8 + 5 = 13 _____   17 − 9 = 8 _____
    14 − 7 = 7 _____   15 − 8 = 7 _____   5 + 9 = 14 _____   5 + 5 = 10 _____

Reviewing rounding, fact families, and inverse operations

Stretch Your Number Sense

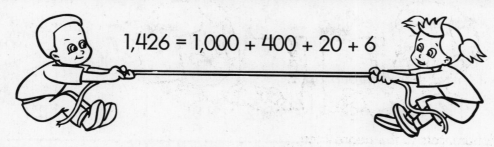

$$1{,}426 = 1{,}000 + 400 + 20 + 6$$

Rewrite each numeral in expanded form.

4,378 _____

6,743 _____

18,734 _____

754,219 _____

Write the numerals in word form.

Example: 7,436 = seven thousand, four hundred thirty-six

9,408 _____

24,972 _____

17,987 _____

64,805 _____

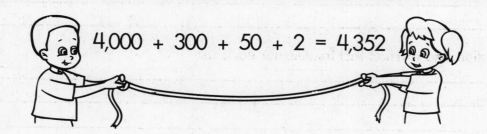

$$4{,}000 + 300 + 50 + 2 = 4{,}352$$

Read the expanded form of the numeral, then write the numeral in standard form.

$10{,}000 + 7{,}000 + 500 + 30 + 2 =$ _____

$6{,}000 + 200 + 40 + 1 =$ _____

$30{,}000 + 1{,}000 + 800 + 60 + 5 =$ _____

$7{,}000 + 400 + 80 + 3 =$ _____

$80{,}000 + 700 + 40 + 9 =$ _____

Writing numerals in standard, word, and expanded form

Numbers Popping Up Everywhere!

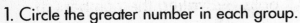

Circle or write the correct answers.

1. Circle the greater number in each group.

3,281	328	429	924	10,582	1,852	214	142
16,927	19,672	752	5,217	3,863	3,683	2,741	742

2. Rewrite the following numbers in order from **greatest** to **least**.

6,791	721	1,403	614	21,572	206

Greatest   Least

_____ _____ _____ _____ _____ _____

3. Make eight different numbers using the digits 7, 4, 1 and 8.
   Write the numbers in order from **greatest** to **least**.

Greatest   Least

8,741 _____ _____ _____ _____ _____ _____ _____

4. Circle the **odd** numbers. Write the **even** numbers on the lines.

27   462   86   2,481   18   124   3   62,400   483   211

_____ _____ _____ _____ _____

5. Continue the patterns.

sixty-three, sixty-five, sixty-seven, _____, _____

2,779   2,782   2,785   2,788 _____, _____, _____

5   8   11   14   17 _____, _____, _____

16   24   32   40 _____, _____, _____

Coach's Helper

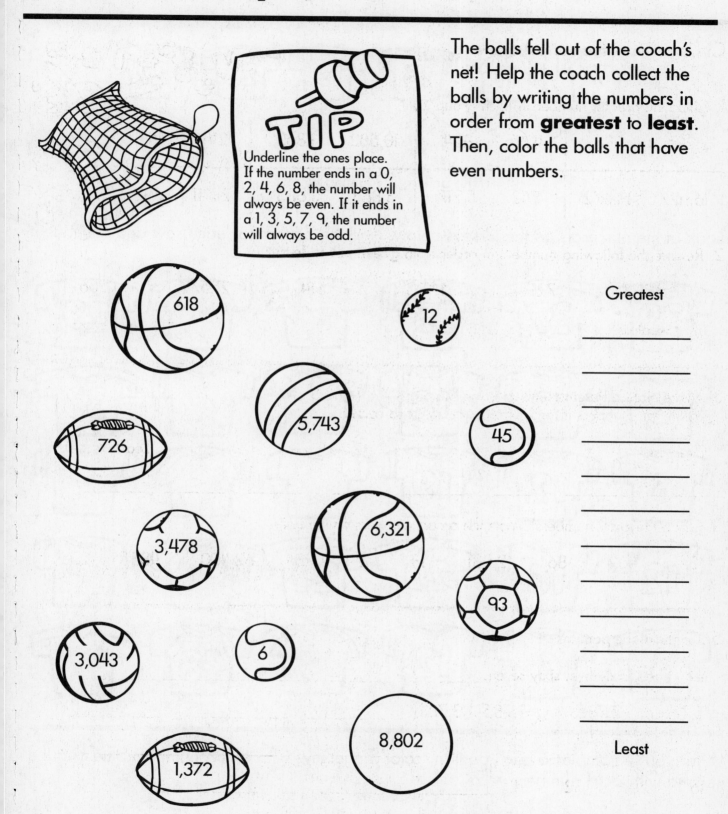

TIP

Underline the ones place. If the number ends in a 0, 2, 4, 6, 8, the number will always be even. If it ends in a 1, 3, 5, 7, 9, the number will always be odd.

The balls fell out of the coach's net! Help the coach collect the balls by writing the numbers in order from **greatest** to **least**. Then, color the balls that have even numbers.

618

12

726

5,743

45

3,478

6,321

93

3,043

6

8,802

1,372

Greatest

_____

_____

_____

_____

_____

_____

_____

_____

_____

_____

Least

Ordering and comparing numbers

5

Winning Patterns

The pattern is counting by 4's!

Look at the numerals on the jerseys below. Find the pattern for each row and continue it.

After you've completed each pattern, color the jerseys with **even** numbers blue and the jerseys with **odd** numbers yellow.

How many **even-numbered** jerseys are there? _____

How many **odd-numbered** jerseys are there? _____

Completing number patterns

Icing the Equations

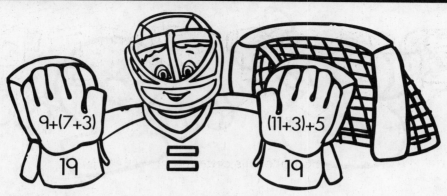

Write the correct symbol (<, >, =, +, −, x, ÷) to make each sentence true.

48 ☐ 62	208 ☐ 179	9 ☐ 5 = 14	7 x 6 ☐ 9 x 9
79 ☐ 7 = 72	4 ☐ 9 = 36	60 ☐ 5 = 12	8 x 6 ☐ 7 x 4
417 ☐ 389 + 28	108 + 9 ☐ 120	40 ☐ 12 x 3	9 x 7 ☐ 12 x 5
573 ☐ 357	306 ☐ 53 = 253	9 x 8 ☐ 12 x 5	32 ÷ 4 ☐ 40 ÷ 5

Write <, >, or = to complete each number sentence.
Remember to do what is in parentheses first!

(12 − 5) +2 ☐ (7 − 5) + 8

7 + (6 x 3) ☐ (4 x 3) + 5

(12 ÷ 6) + 9 ☐ 8 + (24 ÷ 3)

2 + (16 + 3) ☐ (18 + 3) − 8

(6 x 3) + 5 ☐ (14 ÷ 7) + 5

4 + (7 − 2) ☐ 6 + (10 + 5)

(6 x 8) + 2 ☐ (35 − 5) + 10 + 10

5 + 6 + (4 x 5) ☐ (10 − 5) x 5

(13 + 4) − 7 ☐ (7 x 2) + 9

8 + (24 ÷ 6) ☐ 9 x (7 + 4)

(56 ÷ 8) + 12 ☐ 48 + (4 x 3)

5 + (6 x12) ☐ 81 ÷ (16 − 7)

14 + (7 x 3) ☐ 36 − (5 x 3)

36 − (4 x 7) ☐ (9 x 6) - 25

8 x (4 x 2) ☐ (7 x 7) + 15

4 x (6 +3) ☐ 5 + (8 x 2)

Work It Out!

Complete each number sentence using addition, subtraction, multiplication, or division.

Examples: $6 \underline{\,+\,} 2 = 8$ $6 \underline{\,-\,} 2 = 4$ $6 \underline{\,\times\,} 2 = 12$ $6 \underline{\,\div\,} 2 = 3$

$6 \underline{\quad} 7 = 42$

$10 \underline{\quad} 7 = 3$

$15 \underline{\quad} 5 = 10$

$9 \underline{\quad} 8 = 72$

$27 \underline{\quad} 9 = 3$

$12 \underline{\quad} 3 = 15$ $11 \underline{\quad} 4 = 44$

$18 \underline{\quad} 6 = 12$ $23 \underline{\quad} 7 = 16$

$20 \underline{\quad} 5 = 4$ $81 \underline{\quad} 9 = 9$

$16 \underline{\quad} 4 = 4$ $63 \underline{\quad} 7 = 9$

$4 \underline{\quad} 5 = 19$ $8 \underline{\quad} 12 = 96$

$48 \underline{\quad} 6 = 8$ $19 \underline{\quad} 15 = 4$

$42 \underline{\quad} 7 = 6$ $36 \underline{\quad} 6 = 6$

$60 \underline{\quad} 5 = 12$ $23 \underline{\quad} 5 = 28$

$9 \underline{\quad} 7 = 63$

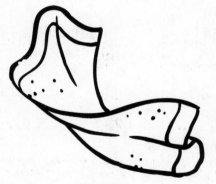

$8 \underline{\quad} 8 = 64$ $21 \underline{\quad} 3 = 7$

$13 \underline{\quad} 6 = 7$ $31 \underline{\quad} 7 = 24$

$23 \underline{\quad} 7 = 30$ $84 \underline{\quad} 7 = 12$

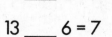

$24 \underline{\quad} 3 = 8$

$27 \underline{\quad} 9 = 18$

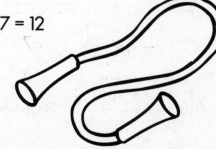

Numbers in Flight

Round the numbers to the nearest tens, hundreds, or thousands.

TIP

Underline the number that holds the rounding place value. Look to the right of the underlined number. If the number is 5 or more, let it soar. If the number is 4 or less, let it rest.

Tens	Hundreds	Thousands
12 _____	418 _____	6,212 _____
26 _____	514 _____	2,578 _____
15 _____	1,232 _____	5,371 _____
367 _____	2,785 _____	9,786 _____
274 _____	6,071 _____	1,321 _____
78 _____	942 _____	4,736 _____
49 _____	237 _____	7,439 _____
63 _____	673 _____	8,742 _____
72 _____	52 _____	9,417 _____
118 _____	3,088 _____	10,714 _____

Keeping Score

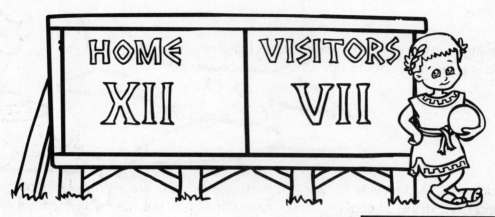

The scores below are written in standard form.
Use the code to write them in Roman numeral form.

Roman Numeral Code

I=1	IV=4	V=5
IX=9	X=10	XV=15
XX=20	XXX=30	XL=40
L=50		

HOME	VISITORS
7	9
___	___

HOME	VISITORS
14	18
___	___

HOME	VISITORS
17	6
___	___

HOME	VISITORS
23	31
___	___

HOME	VISITORS
8	16
___	___

HOME	VISITORS
19	33
___	___

HOME	VISITORS
36	22
___	___

HOME	VISITORS
24	37
___	___

HOME	VISITORS
50	38
___	___

HOME	VISITORS
34	48
___	___

HOME	VISITORS
43	50
___	___

HOME	VISITORS
54	27
___	___

Writing Roman numerals

Story Problem Stumpers!

Solve the problems.

1. Susan is making a list of numbers whose digits have a sum of 20.
   Cross out the number that should not be included on her list.

   5,537   66,404   9,041   992   7,274

2. Mrs. Clayton was buying treats for her children. She bought $12 worth of cinnamon rolls, $9 worth of candy, $8 worth of cookies, and $10 worth of pretzels. Estimate the total amount of money Mrs. Clayton spent.

3. On Friday, 692 people attended a football game at Wyatt Stadium. On Saturday, 934 people attended a soccer game at the same stadium. Estimate how many more people were at the stadium on Saturday than on Friday.

   Approximately how many people were at the stadium on both days combined?

4. The Carter High School Band has been selling raffle tickets for the past four months in order to buy new uniforms. The band sold 2,571 tickets in September, 982 in October, 1,290 in November, and 5,302 in December. Write the amount of tickets sold for the four months in order from greatest to least.

   About how many raffle tickets did the band sell in all?

5. Lacey received a guitar for Christmas. Her goal is to learn to play well by the summer. She practiced her guitar for 7 hours in January, 10 hours in February, and 13 hours in March. If this pattern continues, how many hours will Lacey practice in April?

   How many will she practice in May?

   What is the pattern?

Tasty Treats

Add. Then, use the code to color the treats.

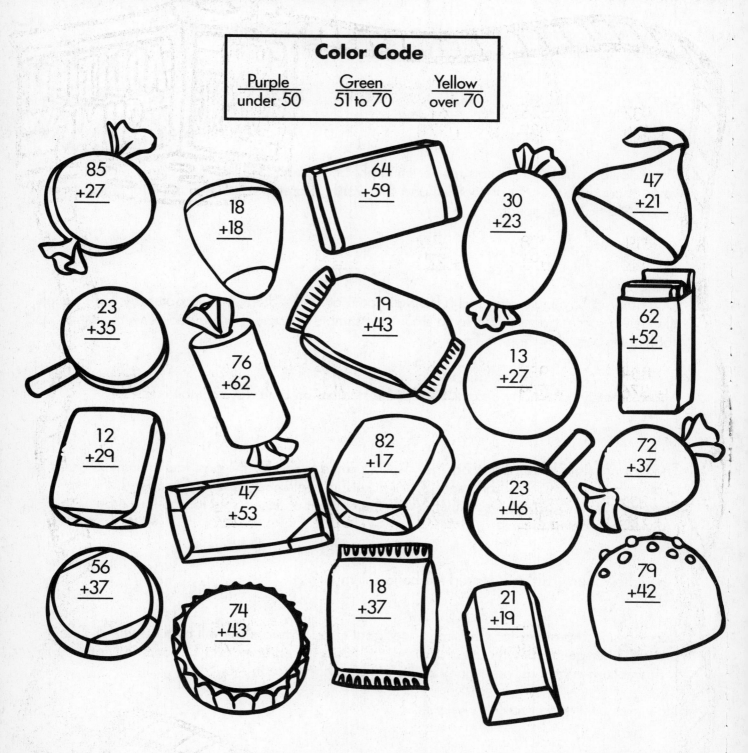

Color Code		
Purple under 50	Green 51 to 70	Yellow over 70

85 +27

18 +18

64 +59

30 +23

47 +21

23 +35

76 +62

19 +43

13 +27

62 +52

12 +29

82 +17

72 +37

47 +53

23 +46

56 +37

74 +43

18 +37

21 +19

79 +42

Adding 2-digit numbers

A Blockbuster Success!

Add. Circle the sums that are **odd** numbers.

437 + 324	526 + 437	612 + 378

619 + 846	708 + 491	792 + 279	437 + 809

884 + 376	987 + 549	807 + 605	989 + 432	643 + 275	650 + 593

322 + 789	403 + 197	737 + 281	812 + 189	283 + 347	527 + 413

803 + 379	902 + 188	543 + 179	817 + 723	425 + 578	275 + 337

Adding 3-digit numbers; identifying odd and even numbers

Sum Popcorn

Add. Mark an **X** on the sum if the number is **even**.

1,598 + 5,269	1,234 + 8,529	6,549 + 3,251	1,224 + 9,872	2,232 + 1,094
1,564 + 6,932	7,727 + 1,236	8,521 + 4,562	2,487 + 4,983	3,987 + 1,870
1,079 + 3,281	2,708 + 1,793	4,805 + 1,389	3,746 + 1,507	5,079 + 1,217
2,748 + 3,005	6,417 + 3,723	9,009 + 2,703	5,408 + 1,783	8,175 + 7,027
6,318 + 1,584	5,726 + 2,375	2,275 + 1,750	3,127 + 1,734	4,025 + 5,140

Adding 4-digit numbers; identifying odd and even numbers

Falling Amounts

Subtract.

938 − 337	657 − 426	549 − 146	486 − 346	748 − 315
432 − 212	860 − 630	354 − 121	762 − 341	388 − 157
576 − 145	927 − 203	659 − 438	284 − 272	743 − 430
767 − 564	849 − 317	983 − 831	454 − 213	788 − 273
939 − 427	748 − 536	965 − 145	847 − 346	876 − 533

Gardening Troubles

Why was the farmer looking for his keys in the garden?

Solve the problems. Then, write the letters below to answer the riddle.

⁴ ¹² 5̶2̶ − 23 **29** T	36 − 27 Y	65 − 48 H	93 − 8 S	71 − 65 I
97 − 59 T	75 − 29 D	85 − 18 H	57 − 49 N	61 − 13 E
68 − 39 O	46 − 18 U	33 − 19 R	56 − 8 E	71 − 15 I
32 − 16 W	41 − 36 H	63 − 38 A	40 − 28 P	51 − 38 N
74 − 25 W	55 − 36 G			

$\overline{67}$ $\overline{48}$ $\overline{49}$ $\overline{25}$ $\overline{85}$ $\overline{5}$ $\overline{29}$ $\overline{12}$ $\overline{6}$ $\overline{8}$ $\overline{19}$ $\overline{29}$ $\overline{17}$ $\overline{48}$ $\overline{9}$ $\overline{46}$

$\overline{38}$ $\overline{28}$ $\overline{14}$ $\overline{13}$ $\overline{56}$ $\overline{12}$.

A Garden of Good Subtraction

Solve the problems. Check your subtraction with addition!

1. $\begin{array}{r} \scriptstyle 2\ 16\ 10\ 12 \\ 3,7\cancel{12} \\ -\ 1,895 \\ \hline 1,817 \end{array}$ $\begin{array}{r} \scriptstyle 1\ \ 1\ 1 \\ 1,817 \\ +\ 1,895 \\ \hline 3,712 \end{array}$	2. $\begin{array}{r} 7,406 \\ -\ 3,677 \\ \hline \end{array}$
3. $\begin{array}{r} 3,413 \\ -\ 1,798 \\ \hline \end{array}$	4. $\begin{array}{r} 5,935 \\ -\ 2,329 \\ \hline \end{array}$
5. $\begin{array}{r} 3,009 \\ -\ 1,998 \\ \hline \end{array}$	6. $\begin{array}{r} 6,187 \\ -\ 2,789 \\ \hline \end{array}$
7. $\begin{array}{r} 4,108 \\ -\ 2,299 \\ \hline \end{array}$	8. $\begin{array}{r} 2,112 \\ -\ \ \ 998 \\ \hline \end{array}$

Round the answers in the subtraction problems to the nearest thousand.

1. _____   2. _____   3. _____   4. _____

5. _____   6. _____   7. _____   8. _____

Shopping Success

Add. Don't forget to line up your decimals!

$148.78 + 16.99	$16.75 + 23.89	$215.89 + 347.23	$107.50 + 341.98
$435.28 + 143.22	$309.78 + 477.45	$706.29 + 88.39	$700.99 + 199.64
$1,079.52 + 8,403.78	$2,783.25 + 103.65	$7,089.18 + 84.23	$2,307.13 + 879.56
$9,078.44 + 3,445.97	$5,655.39 + 1,454.63	$3,905.17 + 7,108.82	$8,805.94 + 6,397.18

After you've solved the problems, do the following. (Round to the nearest thousand.)

1. Circle the sums that can be rounded between $1,000 and $5,000.

2. Mark an **X** on the sums that can be rounded between $6,000 and $10,000.

3. Draw a box around the sums that can be rounded between $11,000 and $15,000.

Fruitful Fun with Decimals

$$\begin{array}{r} 4.927 \\ -\ 1.237 \\ \hline 3.690 \end{array} \longrightarrow \begin{array}{r} 3.690 \\ +\ 1.237 \\ \hline 4.927 \end{array}$$

Remember to line up your decimals!

Subtract. Then, use addition to check your answers.

$\begin{array}{r}1.23\\-\ 0.16\\\hline\end{array}$ + ____	$\begin{array}{r}6.58\\-\ 3.24\\\hline\end{array}$ + ____	$\begin{array}{r}92.36\\-\ 21.55\\\hline\end{array}$ + ____

$\begin{array}{r}2.36\\-\ 1.20\\\hline\end{array}$ + ____	$\begin{array}{r}5.03\\-\ 0.78\\\hline\end{array}$ + ____	$\begin{array}{r}16.25\\-\ 10.16\\\hline\end{array}$ + ____

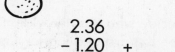

$\begin{array}{r}85.21\\-\ 16.76\\\hline\end{array}$ + ____	$\begin{array}{r}52.89\\-\ 25.13\\\hline\end{array}$ + ____	$\begin{array}{r}17.23\\-\ 16.78\\\hline\end{array}$ + ____

$\begin{array}{r}18.56\\-\ 4.74\\\hline\end{array}$ + ____	$\begin{array}{r}23.79\\-\ 16.83\\\hline\end{array}$ + ____	$\begin{array}{r}43.28\\-\ 15.79\\\hline\end{array}$ + ____

Subtracting decimals; checking subtraction with addition

Story Problems . . . Downloading

Solve the problems.

1. Blaine saw a computer for $475.00 and a printer for $135.00. He decided this was a good deal and just what he needed. In order to buy the computer, Blaine worked each week for three months. He earned $136.00 in March, $231.00 in April, and $179.00 in May. Has Blaine earned enough money to buy the computer and printer? If so, how much will he have left after making the purchase?

2. Lilly was playing a computer game about traveling across the United States. The object of this game is to keep track of the miles traveled. In the first round of the game, Lilly traveled 413 miles. In the second round, she encountered many problems and traveled only 281 miles. She had a successful third round and traveled 674 miles. What is the approximate total number of miles that Lilly traveled in the game?

3. Several of the students in Mrs. Dee's computer class were trying to decide who was the oldest. Carter is younger than Leigh, but older than Kendra. Mark is between Kendra and Carter. List the students from oldest to youngest.

4. The technology students have been studying the rise in population in their city over the past ten years in order to produce graphs. In the first three years, the population increased by 3,716 people. In the next four years, the population went up again by 4,119 people. Finally, in the past three years, it increased by 9,658 people. What is the total number of people the population has increased by over the past ten years?

5. The Cunningham High School Technology Team logs the amount of minutes they spend on the computer each month. In September, they logged 3,107 minutes. In October, they were busy with projects and logged a total of 8,983 minutes for the month. How many more minutes did the technology team log in October than in September?

Solving word problems using addition and subtraction

Multiplication Madness

Complete the multiplication table. Do you see the pattern?

x	1	2	3	4	5	6	7	8	9	10
1	1									
2										
3										
4										
5										
6										
7										
8										
9										
10										

A fact family looks like this: 6 x 7 = 42, 7 x 6 = 42, 42 ÷ 6 = 7, 42 ÷ 7 = 6
Create a fact family using the numbers 2, 5, and 10.

Speeding Along

How fast can you go?

Solve the problems as fast as you can. Time yourself or ask someone to time you.

8 ×3	7 ×9	5 ×3	8 ×7	9 ×3	6 ×5	1 ×9
3 ×4	6 ×6	8 ×9	6 ×4	4 ×9	5 ×7	4 ×5
9 ×5	8 ×8	6 ×7	7 ×9	3 ×8	2 ×2	3 ×2
1 ×3	0 ×9	8 ×6	7 ×3	4 ×4	3 ×3	7 ×3
9 ×9	5 ×4	3 ×9	2 ×7	1 ×8	8 ×5	8 ×2
7 ×7	6 ×3	3 ×2	4 ×0	8 ×4	0 ×8	6 ×0
9 ×7	5 ×2	3 ×6	8 ×9	6 ×7	7 ×2	9 ×3

Time: _____

Number correct: _____ out of 49

Practicing multiplication facts to 9

A Fresh Batch of Multiplication

Step 1:
```
   1
  24     Multiply the ones place first (4 x 4 = 16).
x  4     Write the 6 in the ones place.
   6     Write the 1 ten above so you remember it.
```

Step 2:
```
   1
  24     Now, multiply the tens place
x  4     (2 tens x 4 = 8 tens).
  96     Then, add the 1 ten (1+8=9).
```

Use the steps to cook up some great factors.

Multiply.

```
  12        23        19        14        34        15
x  8      x  9      x  6      x  3      x  6      x  4
```

```
  33        43        29        45        17        35
x  5      x  4      x  2      x  4      x  5      x  8
```

```
  18        13        32        28        42        26
x  3      x  6      x  7      x  3      x  9      x  5
```

```
  25        34        27        16        22        44
x  3      x  4      x  2      x  4      x  7      x  3
```

Multiplying 2-digit numbers by 1-digit numbers with regrouping

Moving Along with Multiplication

High-Flying Multiplication

A. ¹23 x14 **Multiply the ones first.** 2 **Mark the ten you carried.**	B. ¹23 x14 92 **Multiply the tens.**
C. ¹23 x14 92 +230 **Use a 0 to hold the ones place.**	D. 23 x14 92 +230 **Add.** 322

Multiply.

28 x 33	43 x 48	52 x 29	63 x 19	56 x 15
38 x 24	68 x 18	73 x 14	91 x 54	17 x 23
72 x 39	84 x 17	29 x 28	56 x 23	36 x 18
72 x 25	17 x 90	51 x 47	45 x 82	54 x 13

Multiplying 2-digit numbers with regrouping

Fast Forward with Multiplication

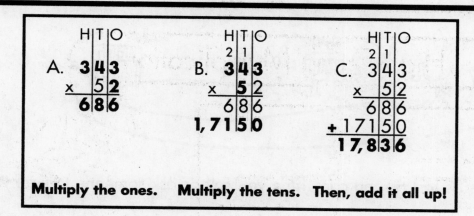

	H	T	O
A.	**3**	**4**	**3**
x		**5**	**2**
	6	**8**	**6**

		2	1
B.	**3**	**4**	**3**
x		**5**	**2**
	6	8	6
1,71		**5**	**0**

		2	1
C.	3	4	3
x		5	2
	6	8	6
+ 17	1	5	0
17,83			**6**

Multiply the ones.   Multiply the tens.   Then, add it all up!

Multiply.

391	478	927	841	614
x 24	x 62	x 45	x 29	x 83

597	658	743	126	239
x 51	x 73	x 16	x 38	x 15

415	807	193	485	318
x 14	x 86	x 19	x 23	x 17

312	451	312	902	605
x 33	x 12	x 50	x 74	x 28

Multiplying 3-digit numbers by 2-digit numbers

And They're Off

Solve the problems as fast as you can. Time yourself or ask someone to time you.

$7\overline{)56}$ $9\overline{)36}$ $6\overline{)42}$ $9\overline{)27}$ $7\overline{)63}$ $4\overline{)24}$ $8\overline{)56}$

$5\overline{)25}$ $8\overline{)0}$ $4\overline{)8}$ $5\overline{)45}$ $4\overline{)28}$ $7\overline{)35}$ $7\overline{)49}$

$9\overline{)18}$ $8\overline{)8}$ $6\overline{)18}$ $7\overline{)14}$ $2\overline{)8}$ $6\overline{)54}$ $9\overline{)18}$

$7\overline{)0}$ $6\overline{)12}$ $3\overline{)6}$ $8\overline{)72}$ $9\overline{)63}$ $3\overline{)24}$ $8\overline{)64}$

$8\overline{)24}$ $5\overline{)40}$ $4\overline{)32}$ $3\overline{)15}$ $6\overline{)30}$ $5\overline{)5}$ $5\overline{)25}$

$4\overline{)4}$ $9\overline{)45}$ $7\overline{)21}$ $8\overline{)40}$ $3\overline{)9}$ $2\overline{)14}$ $9\overline{)72}$

$8\overline{)56}$ $4\overline{)12}$ $2\overline{)0}$ $6\overline{)30}$ $2\overline{)8}$ $8\overline{)48}$ $6\overline{)36}$

Time: _____   Number correct: _____ out of 49

A winner knows that division is the inverse of multiplication.

Leaping Lizards Long Division

It is important to keep all your numbers lined up.

Remember, a quotient is the answer to a division problem.

$$\begin{array}{r} 9\text{r}2 \\ 8\overline{)74} \\ -72 \\ \hline 2 \end{array}$$

Divide to find the quotient. Watch out for remainders!

$7\overline{)49}$ $5\overline{)20}$ $7\overline{)66}$ $8\overline{)47}$ $9\overline{)62}$ $4\overline{)30}$

$2\overline{)14}$ $8\overline{)69}$ $3\overline{)23}$ $7\overline{)42}$ $9\overline{)18}$ $5\overline{)37}$

$9\overline{)88}$ $6\overline{)55}$ $7\overline{)35}$ $7\overline{)53}$ $2\overline{)10}$ $8\overline{)64}$

$2\overline{)16}$ $7\overline{)69}$ $3\overline{)15}$ $4\overline{)35}$ $9\overline{)45}$ $9\overline{)81}$

Dividing 2-digit numbers with and without remainders

Dog Gone Division

Find the quotient!

$$
\begin{array}{r}
114 \\
3\overline{)342} \\
-3\downarrow \\
\hline
4 \\
-3\downarrow \\
\hline
12 \\
-12 \\
\hline
0
\end{array}
$$

Divide.

5⟌655   2⟌144   4⟌364   6⟌240   7⟌455

8⟌224   5⟌235   2⟌122   7⟌560   6⟌552

9⟌279   3⟌156   3⟌189   4⟌428   3⟌753

5⟌425   6⟌456   7⟌126   8⟌656   5⟌630

Take the Challenge!

Divide.

$$217$$
$$7\overline{)1,519}$$
$$-14$$
$$\overline{11}$$
$$-7$$
$$\overline{49}$$
$$-49$$
$$\overline{0}$$

$8\overline{)4,378}$ $4\overline{)2,578}$ $9\overline{)8,327}$ $8\overline{)7,613}$

$6\overline{)3,487}$ $5\overline{)1,575}$ $3\overline{)4,179}$ $6\overline{)1,938}$ $2\overline{)1,675}$

$7\overline{)2,577}$ $8\overline{)2,496}$ $5\overline{)2,673}$ $4\overline{)1,725}$ $3\overline{)2,674}$

Dividing 4-digit numbers with and without remainders

29

Think About It

Solve the problems. Show your work!

1. Kelli bought a new photo album to display her vacation pictures. Each page of the album displays six photos. There are a total of 143 pages in the book. How many photos can the album hold?

   If Kelli has 964 photos, how many more pages does she need?

2. Farmer Joe has many chickens on his farm. Every week he collects and fills 238 cartons of eggs to take to the market. Each carton can hold 12 eggs. What is the total number of eggs that Farmer Joe collects in one week?

3. Sophie enjoys reading. Over the past week and a half, Sophie has read seven books with a total of 966 pages. If all seven books have the same number of pages, which number sentence can be used to find the number of pages in each book?

   a. $966 + 7 =$ ____   b. $966 \times 7 =$ ____   c. $966 \div 7 =$ ____   d. $966 - 7 =$ ____

   How many pages were in each book?

4. Kendra's father is a carpenter. Last week he repaired Mrs. Gibson's deck. He worked for six hours a day for two days until the job was complete. Kendra's father then billed Mrs. Gibson for $45.00 an hour. What was the total amount that Mrs. Gibson had to pay?

5. Jesse had 93 miniature racecars and 87 semi-trucks. The toy tracks that he has will make up ten different roads. Jesse wants to put an equal number of vehicles on each road. How many vehicles can he put on each road?

Solving word problems using multiplication and division

Delicious Fractions

Color the correct amount.

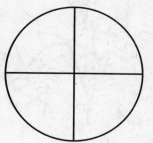 $= \dfrac{3}{4}$

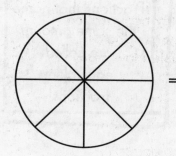 $= \dfrac{3}{8}$

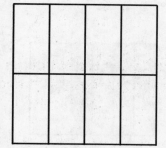 $= \dfrac{4}{8}$

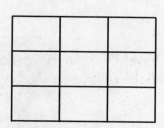 $= \dfrac{3}{9}$

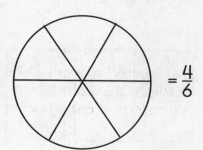 $= \dfrac{4}{6}$

Draw a picture and color part of it to show the fraction.

$\dfrac{7}{8} =$	$\dfrac{4}{10} =$	$\dfrac{3}{5} =$
$\dfrac{2}{5} =$	$\dfrac{2}{7} =$	$\dfrac{5}{6} =$

Fraction Double Take

Write the **equivalent** fraction.

Fractions that name the same amount are called equivalent fractions!

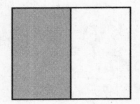 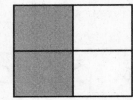

$$\frac{1}{2} = \frac{2}{4}$$

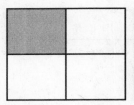 

$$\frac{1}{4} = \frac{}{8}$$

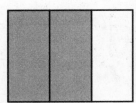 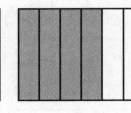

$$\frac{2}{3} = \frac{}{6}$$

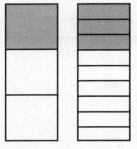

$$\frac{1}{3} = \frac{}{9}$$

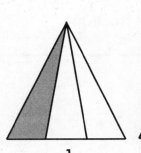

$$\frac{1}{3} = \frac{}{6}$$

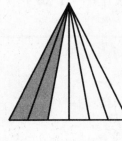

$$\frac{1}{2} = \frac{}{12}$$

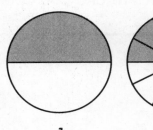 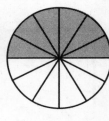

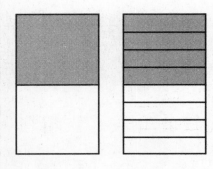

$$\frac{1}{2} = \frac{}{8}$$

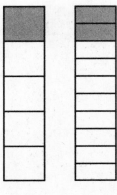

$$\frac{1}{5} = \frac{}{10}$$

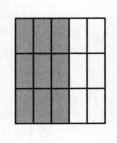 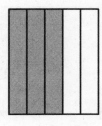

$$\frac{9}{15} = \frac{}{5}$$

Understanding equivalent fractions

Fraction Review I

Shade the correct number of triangles to show the fraction.
Then, write the number that you shaded.

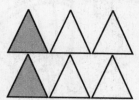

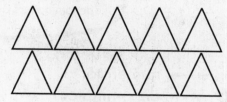

$\frac{1}{3}$ of 6 = _2_

$\frac{1}{5}$ of 10 = ___

$\frac{1}{3}$ of 9 = ___

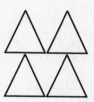

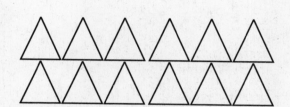

$\frac{1}{2}$ of 4 = ___

$\frac{1}{4}$ of 12 = ___

$\frac{2}{3}$ of 9 = ___

Draw the correct number of circles and shade the number of parts shown.
Then, write the fraction for the shaded area.

6 circles	8 circles	10 circles
3 parts = ___	2 parts = ___	5 parts = ___
12 circles	15 circles	6 circles
4 parts = ___	3 parts = ___	2 parts = ___

Adding it Up

Adding fractions are easy when the denominatiors are the same.

$$\frac{1}{6} + \frac{3}{6} = \frac{4}{6} \longrightarrow \text{numerator} \atop \longrightarrow \text{denominator}$$

Add.

$\dfrac{2}{6} + \dfrac{4}{6} =$ 　　　　　$\dfrac{1}{5} + \dfrac{1}{5} =$ 　　　　　$\dfrac{4}{16} + \dfrac{7}{16} =$

$\dfrac{6}{10} + \dfrac{3}{10} =$ 　　　　　$\dfrac{1}{9} + \dfrac{6}{9} =$ 　　　　　$\dfrac{5}{8} + \dfrac{2}{8} =$

$\dfrac{5}{9} + \dfrac{1}{9} =$ 　　　　　$\dfrac{2}{7} + \dfrac{1}{7} =$ 　　　　　$\dfrac{2}{6} + \dfrac{3}{6} =$

$\dfrac{2}{10} + \dfrac{7}{10} =$ 　　　　　$\dfrac{1}{12} + \dfrac{3}{12} =$ 　　　　　$\dfrac{3}{9} + \dfrac{4}{9} =$

$\dfrac{3}{8} + \dfrac{5}{8} =$ 　　　　　$\dfrac{3}{5} + \dfrac{1}{5} =$ 　　　　　$\dfrac{5}{12} + \dfrac{6}{12} =$

$\dfrac{7}{16} + \dfrac{4}{16} =$ 　　　　　$\dfrac{5}{10} + \dfrac{3}{10} =$ 　　　　　$\dfrac{6}{14} + \dfrac{1}{14} =$

$\dfrac{4}{8} + \dfrac{2}{8} =$ 　　　　　$\dfrac{3}{15} + \dfrac{7}{15} =$ 　　　　　$\dfrac{3}{12} + \dfrac{7}{12} =$

Fraction Review II

Solve the fraction problems. Remember to watch your signs.

$\frac{1}{6} + \frac{2}{6} = \frac{3}{6}$

$\frac{3}{5} - \frac{1}{5} =$

$\frac{5}{12} + \frac{6}{12} =$

$\frac{5}{9} + \frac{1}{9} =$

$\frac{7}{10} + \frac{2}{10} =$

$\frac{6}{12} - \frac{2}{12} =$

$\frac{7}{9} - \frac{5}{9} =$

$\frac{9}{10} - \frac{5}{10} =$

$\frac{2}{3} - \frac{1}{3} =$

$\frac{7}{8} - \frac{3}{8} =$

$\frac{3}{7} + \frac{1}{7} =$

$\frac{5}{8} + \frac{2}{8} =$

$\frac{4}{16} + \frac{4}{16} =$

$\frac{8}{12} + \frac{2}{12} =$

$\frac{9}{12} - \frac{4}{12} =$

$\frac{7}{10} - \frac{4}{10} =$

$\frac{6}{9} + \frac{2}{9} =$

$\frac{8}{16} - \frac{4}{16} =$

$\frac{5}{15} + \frac{10}{15} =$

$\frac{7}{16} - \frac{5}{16} =$

$\frac{9}{12} + \frac{2}{12} =$

Fun with Fractions

Finding the greatest common factors for both numbers can be easy!

Simplify those fractions!

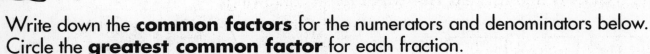

$\frac{8}{32}$ List all the factors that equal the numerator! (1,2,4,⑧)

List all the factors that equal the denominator! (1,2,4,⑧,32)

Now, circle the greatest common factor!

Write down the **common factors** for the numerators and denominators below.
Circle the **greatest common factor** for each fraction.

$\frac{6}{18}$ $\frac{6}{24}$ $\frac{9}{36}$ $\frac{7}{42}$

_____   _____   _____   _____

_____   _____   _____   _____

$\frac{9}{81}$ $\frac{8}{48}$ $\frac{12}{36}$ $\frac{14}{28}$

_____   _____   _____   _____

_____   _____   _____   _____

Example: $\frac{3 \div 3}{6 \div 3} = \frac{1}{2}$ 1st – Find the greatest common factor of the numerator and denominator.
2nd – Divide both the numerator and denominator by that number.

Congratulations! You've just simplified that fraction!

Simplify the fractions.

$\frac{4}{12}$ = _____ $\frac{5}{25}$ = _____ $\frac{7}{28}$ = _____ $\frac{6}{48}$ = _____ $\frac{8}{72}$ = _____

$\frac{12}{24}$ = _____ $\frac{14}{21}$ = _____ $\frac{4}{32}$ = _____ $\frac{7}{63}$ = _____ $\frac{9}{36}$ = _____

$\frac{3}{18}$ = _____ $\frac{9}{27}$ = _____ $\frac{6}{12}$ = _____ $\frac{12}{48}$ = _____ $\frac{9}{12}$ = _____

$\frac{5}{20}$ = _____ $\frac{8}{16}$ = _____ $\frac{7}{21}$ = _____ $\frac{16}{48}$ = _____ $\frac{12}{18}$ = _____

Simplifying fractions

Different, but the SAME!

Write the **fraction** and **mixed numeral** for the following:

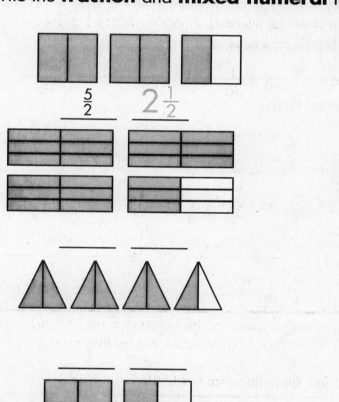

$$\frac{5}{2} \qquad 2\frac{1}{2}$$

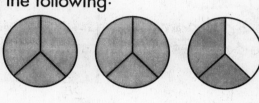

_____ _____

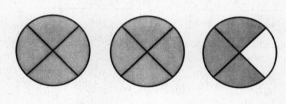

_____ _____

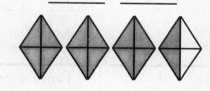

_____ _____

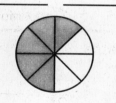

_____ _____

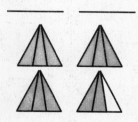

_____ _____

That's Top Heavy

Write the mixed number as an **improper fraction**.

$2\frac{3}{4} = \frac{11}{4}$ $6\frac{4}{5} =$ $8\frac{4}{7} =$

$4\frac{5}{8} =$ $7\frac{3}{7} =$ $5\frac{2}{9} =$

$8\frac{3}{4} =$ $5\frac{1}{2} =$ $3\frac{4}{8} =$

$3\frac{2}{9} =$ $7\frac{5}{9} =$ $7\frac{2}{4} =$

$2\frac{1}{4} =$ $2\frac{3}{7} =$ $3\frac{5}{7} =$

$5\frac{3}{8} =$ $4\frac{1}{6} =$ $1\frac{7}{9} =$

$5\frac{2}{8} =$ $6\frac{3}{5} =$ $8\frac{3}{5} =$

$1\frac{5}{9} =$ $8\frac{4}{9} =$ $2\frac{7}{8} =$

What's the Value?

$$\underset{\text{Hundreds}}{\underline{\hspace{1cm}}} \quad \underset{\text{Tens}}{\underline{\hspace{1cm}}} \quad \underset{\text{Ones}}{\underline{\textbf{0}}} \, \bullet \, \underset{\text{Tenths}}{\underline{\textbf{2}}} \quad \underset{\text{Hundredths}}{\underline{\hspace{1cm}}} = \frac{2}{10}$$

Decimal

A decimal is a number that uses place value and a decimal point to show value less than a whole (or one).

A fraction does the same thing. So fractions and decimals mean the same thing. They are just written a little differently.

This whole is divided into tenths.

$$\frac{2}{10} = 0.2$$

This whole is divided into hundredths.

$$0.26 = \frac{26}{100}$$

Write the **fraction** and the **decimal** for each.

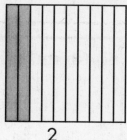 _____ = _____   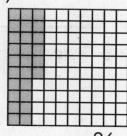 _____ = _____

 _____ = _____   _____ = _____

  _____ = _____   _____ = _____

 _____ = _____   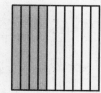 _____ = _____

Understanding fractions and decimals

39

Changing Units

The Golden Rule
When you change larger units to smaller units, you multiply.
Example: 4 yards x 3 feet = 12 feet
When you change smaller units to larger units, you divide.
Example: 36 inches ÷ 12 feet = 3 feet

Convert each unit of measure.

Customary Units for Linear Measures
12 inches = 1 foot
3 feet = 1 yard
5,280 feet = 1 mile
1,760 yards = 1 mile

9 feet = _____ yards

36 inches = _____ yards

48 inches = _____ feet

7 feet = _____ inches

36 feet = _____ yards

3,520 yards = _____ miles

5 yards = _____ feet

6 feet = _____ yards

3 miles = _____ feet

14 feet = _____ inches

6 yards = _____ inches

21 feet = _____ yards

2 miles = _____ feet

9 yards = _____ feet

60 inches = _____ feet

96 inches = _____ feet

12 yards = _____ inches

144 inches = _____ feet

5 miles = _____ feet

12 feet = _____ inches

9 miles = _____ yards

2 miles = _____ feet

30 yards = _____ feet

10 yards = _____ inches

9 feet = _____ inches

3 miles = _____ yards

18 yards = _____ inches

46 feet = _____ inches

48 feet = _____ yards

72 inches = _____ feet

24 feet = _____ yards

84 inches = _____ feet

4 miles = _____ feet

If fencing is $2.00 per foot, how much would it cost to fence a dog run with a 36-yard perimeter for Brutus to have fun in?

Understanding linear units of measure

The Rule of Thumb

Remember to multiply when you change larger units to smaller units and to divide when you change smaller units to larger units.

Customary Units for Measuring Liquids	Customary Units For Measuring Weight
1 pint = 2 cups (c.) 1 quart = 2 pints (pt.) 1 gallon = 4 quarts (qt.)	16 ounces (oz) = 1 pound (lb.) 2,000 lbs = 1 ton (T.)

Circle the more reasonable measurement.

300 T. or 300 lbs.

4 oz. or 4 lbs.

14 oz. or 14 lbs.

10 lbs. or 10 T.

15 T. or 15 lbs.

1 lb. or 1 oz.

15 lb. or 15 oz.

Convert each unit of measure.

8 cups = _____ qt.   2 lb = _____ oz.   3 pt = _____ c.

3 gal = _____ qt.   64 oz = _____ lb.   2 gal = _____ pt.

1 qt = _____ c.   4 T = _____ lb.   3 qt = _____ c.

12 pt = _____ c.   3 lbs = _____ oz.   8 lb = _____ oz.

3 qt = _____ c.   6 pt = _____ c.   5 gal = _____ qt.

Tony needs four cups of cream for a pie. The store sells cream in one-pint containers. How many pints should Tony buy?

Where in the World

Customary Units For Measuring Time
60 seconds = 1 minute
60 minutes = 1 hour
24 hours = 1 day

Solve the problems.

1. Clay spends seven hours each day at school. He goes to school Monday through Friday. About how many hours does Clay spend at school in one week?

2. Craig's guitar lessons were two hours long. If his lesson ended at 6:15, what time did it begin?

3. Cheryl spent the day cleaning. It took her 25 minutes to vacuum, 18 minutes to dust, and 90 minutes to do the laundry. How many minutes did she spend cleaning?

   How many hours?

4. Barbara exercised for 24 minutes. Then she watched television for 40 minutes. Did the two activities combined take more or less than an hour?

5. Abbey sleeps for ten hours. Then she takes her friends to the mall for six hours and the water park for seven hours. Finally, Abbey spends two hours eating meals and helping her mom around the house. Will she be able to do everything in one day? Explain your answer.

Challenge yourself!
Create a list of things that you do that take a second, minute, hour, or day.

Understanding time units of measure; solving word problems

Elapsed Time

Saturday Movie Times at Cinema Town

10:00 a.m.	Smokey Town
11:45 a.m.	The Pink Cat
12:15 p.m.	Julie's Wish
3:30 p.m.	Emma's Challenge

What time does it start?

1. All the movies last 2 hours and 10 minutes. What time will each movie end?

2. If Elizabeth had to walk home after the 3:30 p.m. showing of Emma's Challenge and it took her 20 minutes to walk home, what time would she get home?

3. Lloyd arrived at Cinema Town at 9:00 a.m. He was able to stay long enough to watch Smokey Town and Emma's Challenge. How long did Lloyd stay at the movies?

4. How much time is there between the end of The Pink Cat and the beginning of Emma's Challenge?

5. Don and Mark are going to the movies. The movie theater is closer to Mark's house and it takes 15 minutes to get there. If it takes Don 10 minutes to walk to Mark's house and they want to leave in time to see The Pink Cat, what time will Don need to leave his house?

Complete the charts.

Start Time	End Time	Elapsed Time
1:15 a.m.	_____	50 min.
7:30 a.m.	5:25 p.m.	_____

Start Time	End Time	Elapsed Time
1:30 p.m.	2:40 p.m.	_____
3:45 p.m.	5:15 p.m.	_____

Start Time	End Time	Elapsed Time
7:30 p.m.	_____	1 hr., 13 min.
8:15 p.m.	_____	40 min.

Start Time	End Time	Elapsed Time
2:15 p.m.	7:30 p.m.	_____
5:45 p.m.	_____	1 hr., 20 min.

Perimeter, It's What's Around You!

Perimeter is the distance around a figure.
To find the perimeter of a shape or figure,
add all the sides.

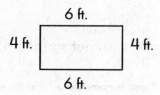

6 ft.
4 ft.   4 ft.
6 ft.

4 ft. + 4 ft. = 8 ft. and 6 ft. + 6 ft. = 12 ft.
OR
4 ft. x 2 sides = 8 ft. and 6 ft. x 2 sides = 12 ft.

8 ft. + 12 ft. = 20 ft. perimeter

Hmm...?

Find the **perimeter** of each shape.

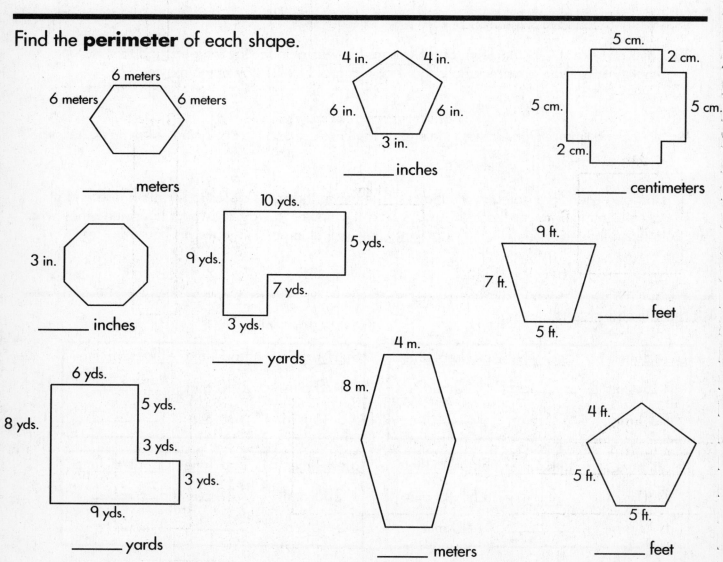

6 meters
6 meters   6 meters

_____ meters

4 in.   4 in.
6 in.   6 in.
3 in.

_____ inches

5 cm.
2 cm.
5 cm.   5 cm.
2 cm.

_____ centimeters

3 in.

_____ inches

10 yds.
5 yds.
9 yds.
7 yds.
3 yds.

_____ yards

9 ft.
7 ft.
5 ft.

_____ feet

6 yds.
5 yds.
8 yds.
3 yds.
3 yds.
9 yds.

_____ yards

4 m.
8 m.

_____ meters

4 ft.
5 ft.
5 ft.

_____ feet

Awesome Amounts of Area

Area is the amount of square units needed (or used) to cover a flat surface.

Area = Length x Width

Find the **area** of each. Write the equation and the answer.

4 in.

10 in.

$10 \times 4 = 40$ in.

6 ft.

8 ft.

2 cm.

10 cm.

_____

8 m.

8 m.

9 km.

2 km.

3 yds.

12 yds.

_____

_____

_____

13 in.

3 in.

_____

24 yds.

12 yds.

5 m.

10 m.

_____

_____

Amazing Angles

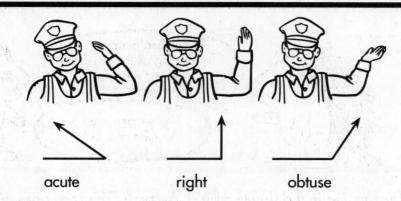

acute   right   obtuse

Write the name of each angle.

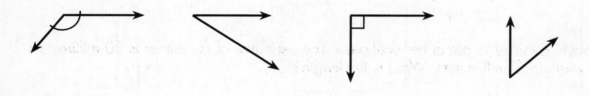

_____   _____   _____   _____

Write the name of the marked angle.

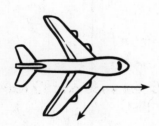

_____   _____

How many of each angle can you find on the house?

____ acute   ____ right   ____ obtuse

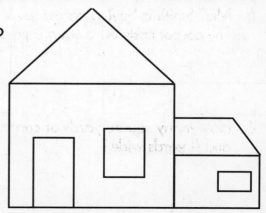

Measuring Around

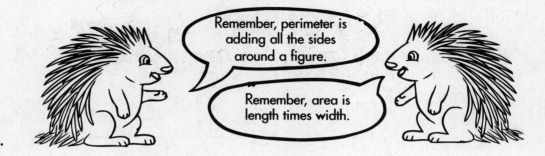

Remember, perimeter is adding all the sides around a figure.

Remember, area is length times width.

Solve the problems.

1. On Saturday, Kris is running in the 4-mile race at the park. The race goes around the park two times. The park is a square. What is the length of each side?

2. Katie bought a mirror to put in her dollhouse. The perimeter of the mirror is 50 millimeters and the width is 10 millimeters. What is the length?

3. Mike wants to make a fence for his garden. The garden is 24 feet long and 16 feet wide. How much fence does Mike need to buy?

4. Stella loves to go to the art museum. Her favorite painting is 25 feet wide and 10 feet tall. What is the area of the painting?

5. Mrs. Smith is buying carpet for a small room in her house. She needs 9 square yards. The carpet costs $5 a square yard. How much will Mrs. Smith pay for the carpet?

6. How many square yards of carpet do you need to cover a floor that is 6 yards long and 4 yards wide?

Rounding Numbers

Round the numbers to the nearest **ten**.

248 _____   63 _____   71 _____   326 _____   104 _____

97 _____   56 _____   1,247 _____   83 _____   653 _____

45 _____   132 _____   87 _____   49 _____   99 _____

354 _____   16 _____   308 _____   757 _____   37 _____

Round the numbers to the nearest **hundred**.

3,743 _____   12,278 _____   374 _____   145 _____

546 _____   2,453 _____   98 _____   4,389 _____

2,614 _____   194 _____   7,643 _____   893 _____

216 _____   673 _____   1,783 _____   574 _____

Round the numbers to the nearest **thousand**.

17,524 _____   6,429 _____   3,941 _____   2,642 _____

4,834 _____   4,216 _____   1,823 _____   9,487 _____

23,573 _____   6,840 _____   7,927 _____   1,431 _____

16,743 _____   5,327 _____   9,849 _____   3,347 _____

Rounding numbers to tens, hundreds, and thousands

Addition Review

Add.

$$
\begin{array}{r} 258 \\ + 31 \\ \hline \end{array}
\qquad
\begin{array}{r} 368 \\ + 527 \\ \hline \end{array}
\qquad
\begin{array}{r} 57 \\ + 36 \\ \hline \end{array}
\qquad
\begin{array}{r} 845 \\ + 445 \\ \hline \end{array}
\qquad
\begin{array}{r} 1,684 \\ + 459 \\ \hline \end{array}
$$

$$
\begin{array}{r} 245 \\ + 124 \\ \hline \end{array}
\qquad
\begin{array}{r} 681 \\ + 110 \\ \hline \end{array}
\qquad
\begin{array}{r} 1,765 \\ + 4,730 \\ \hline \end{array}
\qquad
\begin{array}{r} 752 \\ + 774 \\ \hline \end{array}
\qquad
\begin{array}{r} 26 \\ + 64 \\ \hline \end{array}
$$

$$
\begin{array}{r} 560 \\ + 230 \\ \hline \end{array}
\qquad
\begin{array}{r} 48 \\ + 99 \\ \hline \end{array}
\qquad
\begin{array}{r} 3,287 \\ + 1,721 \\ \hline \end{array}
\qquad
\begin{array}{r} 664 \\ + 201 \\ \hline \end{array}
\qquad
\begin{array}{r} 231 \\ + 421 \\ \hline \end{array}
$$

$$
\begin{array}{r} 76 \\ + 23 \\ \hline \end{array}
\qquad
\begin{array}{r} 579 \\ + 457 \\ \hline \end{array}
\qquad
\begin{array}{r} 7,580 \\ + 1,478 \\ \hline \end{array}
\qquad
\begin{array}{r} 305 \\ + 185 \\ \hline \end{array}
\qquad
\begin{array}{r} 1,400 \\ + 2,624 \\ \hline \end{array}
$$

$$
\begin{array}{r} 309 \\ + 326 \\ \hline \end{array}
\qquad
\begin{array}{r} 1,486 \\ + 2,006 \\ \hline \end{array}
\qquad
\begin{array}{r} 47 \\ + 32 \\ \hline \end{array}
\qquad
\begin{array}{r} 6,078 \\ + 1,033 \\ \hline \end{array}
\qquad
\begin{array}{r} 1,985 \\ + 2,191 \\ \hline \end{array}
$$

Multiplication Review I

Multiply.

9 ×7	8 ×7	6 ×5	4 ×3	5 ×8	6 ×7
4 ×7	6 ×6	5 ×7	6 ×3	9 ×4	8 ×3
7 ×7	3 ×7	9 ×5	8 ×8	5 ×6	7 ×9
6 ×6	9 ×9	5 ×5	8 ×4	7 ×6	3 ×4
6 ×9	8 ×5	5 ×4	9 ×7	7 ×8	8 ×9
4 ×6	8 ×6	9 ×3	7 ×4	9 ×5	3 ×5

Reviewing multiplication facts to 9

Multiplication Review II

Multiply.

12 × 39	23 × 7	37 × 52	49 × 4	33 × 18	22 × 7
83 × 8	92 × 81	79 × 8	57 × 16	85 × 4	45 × 17
57 × 19	63 × 3	74 × 31	67 × 6	23 × 14	24 × 9
19 × 7	21 × 89	39 × 5	48 × 52	71 × 7	83 × 14
52 × 27	18 × 6	38 × 29	47 × 3	52 × 13	13 × 9
41 × 8	67 × 18	79 × 3	83 × 19	93 × 5	57 × 12

Multiplication Review III

Multiply.

Remember: Multiply the ones place first. Multiply the tens place second.
Then, add them together!

613 x 42	459 x 17	931 x 31	372 x 18	492 x 22
785 x 73	412 x 16	396 x 89	137 x 45	209 x 29
917 x 64	406 x 92	381 x 57	710 x 27	118 x 72
814 x 74	926 x 28	231 x 13	174 x 40	349 x 29
905 x 81	714 x 39	817 x 48	273 x 12	384 x 17

Reviewing multiplication

Division Review I

Divide.

$2\overline{)4}$ $9\overline{)18}$ $9\overline{)72}$ $9\overline{)0}$ $6\overline{)36}$ $3\overline{)15}$ $4\overline{)20}$

$7\overline{)63}$ $9\overline{)81}$ $2\overline{)14}$ $5\overline{)10}$ $3\overline{)6}$ $2\overline{)2}$ $7\overline{)35}$

$8\overline{)56}$ $7\overline{)49}$ $5\overline{)50}$ $7\overline{)14}$ $5\overline{)25}$ $2\overline{)18}$ $4\overline{)36}$

$8\overline{)72}$ $4\overline{)28}$ $4\overline{)20}$ $5\overline{)30}$ $9\overline{)0}$ $3\overline{)6}$ $9\overline{)81}$

$9\overline{)54}$ $4\overline{)16}$ $9\overline{)63}$ $5\overline{)35}$ $8\overline{)16}$ $9\overline{)45}$ $5\overline{)5}$

$2\overline{)12}$ $7\overline{)14}$ $6\overline{)6}$ $5\overline{)0}$ $7\overline{)49}$ $8\overline{)40}$ $7\overline{)70}$

$3\overline{)12}$ $9\overline{)63}$ $4\overline{)32}$ $3\overline{)21}$ $8\overline{)8}$ $5\overline{)0}$ $2\overline{)14}$

Division Review II

Divide.

$7\overline{)91}$ $6\overline{)84}$ $4\overline{)97}$ $5\overline{)75}$ $2\overline{)82}$ $3\overline{)78}$

$3\overline{)72}$ $4\overline{)68}$ $5\overline{)65}$ $2\overline{)72}$ $5\overline{)70}$ $7\overline{)84}$

$6\overline{)93}$ $7\overline{)97}$ $8\overline{)96}$ $3\overline{)81}$ $4\overline{)98}$ $8\overline{)93}$

$2\overline{)98}$ $4\overline{)76}$ $3\overline{)57}$ $5\overline{)92}$ $6\overline{)78}$ $6\overline{)72}$

$2\overline{)88}$ $3\overline{)69}$ $7\overline{)91}$ $6\overline{)83}$ $4\overline{)94}$ $5\overline{)99}$

Reviewing 2-digit long division

Division Review III

Divide.

8$\overline{)729}$ 6$\overline{)375}$ 7$\overline{)575}$ 9$\overline{)817}$ 3$\overline{)472}$

4$\overline{)159}$ 8$\overline{)928}$ 5$\overline{)318}$ 7$\overline{)287}$ 7$\overline{)523}$

3$\overline{)870}$ 9$\overline{)760}$ 6$\overline{)642}$ 5$\overline{)973}$ 9$\overline{)387}$

4$\overline{)732}$ 6$\overline{)849}$ 8$\overline{)417}$ 7$\overline{)917}$ 6$\overline{)748}$

Let Your Brilliance Shine!

1. Write the numbers using Roman numerals

   66 _____   47 _____

2.
   4,793   3,482
   + 349   - 684

3. (4 x 7) – 4 ___ 8 + (6 x 5)

   ○ a. ÷   ○ b. <

   ○ c. =   ○ d. >

4. Round the numbers to the nearest thousand.

   7,434   2,921   1,682

   _____   _____   _____

5. 4,609.72 – 526.94 = _____

   ○ a. 4,082.73   ○ b. 4,083.78

   ○ c. 4,082.78   ○ d. 4,183.78

6. 84 ÷ 9 = _____

   ○ a. 850   ○ b. 92 r13

   ○ c. 91 r4   ○ d. 93 r4

7. Write the standard form of three million, forty-six thousand, eight hundred three.

8. Write the word form for 5,870,403.

9. Todd's four friends have no sports trading cards of their own. Todd has 246 baseball cards and 134 football cards. He would like to share his cards with his friends. How many cards will Todd and each of his friends receive? Will they all receive the same amount?

10. Priscilla and her three friends like to play with dolls at her house. She has quite a collection and always likes to share evenly. Priscilla has 76 dolls. She wants each person to have the same number of dolls. How many will each person get? Will there be any dolls left over?

11. Kyle feeds his dog Skippy twice a day. Skippy eats one cup of food each time he is fed. How many cups of food will Skippy eat in a four-week period?

Show What You Know!

---

1. Find the missing number in this pattern.

    176, 171, _____, 161, 156

   ○ a. 169   ○ b. 166

   ○ c. 170   ○ d. 165

2.

   187   904
   x 92   x 76

---

3. I am > 634.
   I am even.
   My digits total 17.
   What number am I?

   ○ a. 619   ○ b. 638   ○ c. 736   ○ d. 566

4. Round the numbers to the nearest hundred.

   3,709   8,324   7,641

   _____   _____   _____

---

5. 132.78 + 8,746.23 = _____

6. 9,756 ÷ 8 = _____

---

7. Write the expanded form of 8,746.

8. 4 hundreds + 11 tens + 7 ones = _____

   ○ a. 417   ○ b. 418

   ○ c. 517   ○ d. 507

---

9. Jill saved her babysitting money for several months. She has a total of $89.75 and is going to buy a portable CD player for $37.95 and a CD for $15.99. How much money will Jill have left?

10. Chad sells newspapers. He delivered 378 papers on Monday, 264 papers on Tuesday, and 418 papers on Wednesday. About how many papers has Chad delivered so far this week?

11. Lacey was cleaning her family's closets and found they had a total of 31 pairs of shoes. After talking with the girls at school, she found that Christina's family has 47 pairs of shoes and Emily's small family has 26 pairs of shoes. What method could be used to find how many more pairs of shoes Christina's family has than Emily's family?

   ○ a. Add 31 and 26.   ○ b. Subtract 31 from 47.

   ○ c. Add 26 and 31 and subtract the sum from 47.   ○ d. Subtract 26 from 47.

Applying math skills

Fractions and Decimals

Numbers less than a whole can be written two ways—as a fraction or as a decimal. Rewrite the numbers as fractions or decimals.

$\frac{2}{10}$ = _____ $\frac{40}{100}$ = _____ $\frac{8}{10}$ = _____

0.9 = _____   0.46 = _____   0.79 = _____

$\frac{53}{100}$ = _____ $\frac{3}{10}$ = _____ $\frac{31}{100}$ = _____

56 = _____   0.7 = _____   0.5 = _____

$\frac{6}{10}$ = _____ $\frac{28}{100}$ = _____ $\frac{1}{10}$ = _____

0.83 = _____   0.98 = _____   0.4 = _____

$\frac{62}{100}$ = _____   0.92 = _____ $\frac{43}{100}$ = _____

$\frac{7}{10}$ = _____   0.37 = _____ $\frac{18}{100}$ = _____

0.51 = _____ $\frac{27}{100}$ = _____   0.82 = _____

$\frac{3}{10}$ = _____   0.8 = _____ $\frac{19}{100}$ = _____

0.21 = _____ $\frac{79}{100}$ = _____   0.13 = _____

$\frac{63}{100}$ = _____   0.43 = _____ $\frac{74}{100}$ = _____

Mixed Review I

1. Which is the most likely to have the capacity of a gallon?

   ○ a. kitchen sink   ○ b. water jug
   ○ c. bath tub   ○ d. soda can

2. A bathtub would have the capacity of:

   ○ a. 3 gallons   ○ b. 4 pints
   ○ c. 50 liters   ○ d. 1 cup

3. Grandma was in the baking mood. She decided to make a cake for each of her five grandchildren. Each cake called for eight ounces of cocoa. How many ounces of cocoa did grandma have to buy?

4. Bill needs his morning coffee. If his coffee pot holds one quart of coffee and he pours himself one cup. How much is in the pot now?

5. An elephant would be measured in what?

   ○ a. pounds   ○ b. tons
   ○ c. millimeters   ○ d. gallons

6. An encyclopedia would be weighed in what?

   ○ a. grams   ○ b. kilograms

   If one encyclopedia weighed 2 _____, how much would 8 weigh?

7. Tim has a bag of marbles that weighs 18 grams. If Jeff's bag of marbles weighs 27 grams, how much more does Jeff's bag weigh than Tim's?

8. If a new born baby weighs 7 lbs., how many ounces is that?

9. Lacey and Tim competed in a dance marathon. They danced for a total of 4 hours and 28 minutes. How many **minutes** did Lacey and Tim dance?

   ○ a. 240 min.   ○ b. 258 min.
   ○ c. 158 min.   ○ d. 268 min.

10. Beth checked out a new book from the library. She just couldn't put it down. She read for a total of 1 hour and 57 minutes yesterday and finished it today by reading for 48 minutes. How many total hours and minutes did it take her to read the book?

Mixed Review II

Solve the problems.

1. Round 564 to the nearest ten.

   ○ a. 570   ○ b. 565   ○ c. 560   ○ d. 600

2. Round 5,758 to the nearest hundred.

   ○ a. 6,000   ○ b. 5,800   ○ c. 5,760   ○ d. 5,700

3. Alora bought eight hair ribbons. Each ribbon was 18 inches long. How many yards of ribbon did Alora purchase?

   ○ a. 8 yds. 9 in.   ○ b. 9 yds.
   ○ c. 11 yds. 10 in.   ○ d. 4 yds.

4. The circus ran out of pennies and nickels to make change so it had to round everything to the nearest $0.10. What will a $0.78 item cost?

   ○ a. $0.75   ○ b. $0.80
   ○ c. $1.00   ○ d. $0.70

5.
   $$578 \times 27$$
   $$693 \times 48$$

6. $278 \div 4 =$ $3,764 \div 8 =$

7. How much of the pizza has been eaten? Simplify your fraction.

8. Karen is older than David. Mark is older than Karen. Angie is older Mark. Who is the oldest?

9. Connie has a doctor's appointment at 3:30 p.m. She was held up at school and didn't arrive until 4:50 p.m. How late was Connie?

10. Find the greatest common factor for each fraction and simplify.

    $$\frac{16}{64} = \underline{\quad}$$ $$\frac{9}{54} = \underline{\quad}$$ $$\frac{25}{45} = \underline{\quad}$$

Applying math skills

Answer Key

Please take time to review the work your child has completed and remember to praise both success and effort. If your child makes a mistake, let him or her know that mistakes are a part of learning. Then explain the correct answer and how to find it. Taking the time to help your child and an active interest in his or her progress shows that you feel learning is important.

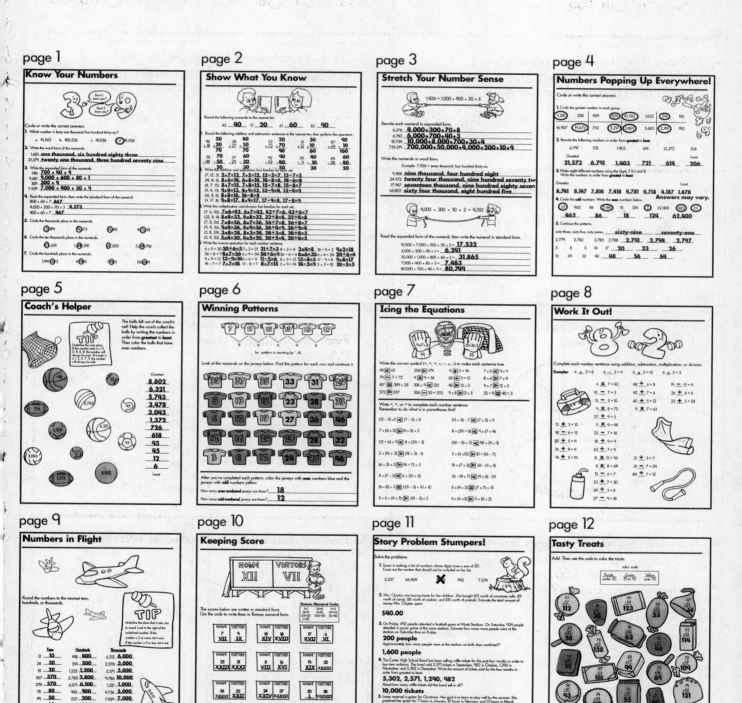

A Blockbuster Success!

Add. Circle the sums that are odd numbers.

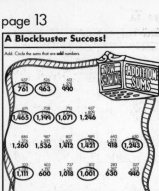

| 437 | 526 | 612 |
| 761 | 963 | 990 |

| 618 | 708 | 792 | 437 |
| 1,465 | 1,199 | 1,071 | 1,246 |

| 884 | 987 | 807 | 486 | 643 | 650 |
| 1,260 | 1,536 | 1,412 | 1,421 | 918 | 1,243 |

| 322 | 403 | 737 | 812 | 283 | 527 |
| 1,111 | 600 | 1,018 | 1,001 | 630 | 440 |

| 803 | 902 | 543 | 817 | 425 | 275 |
| 1,182 | 1,090 | 722 | 1,540 | 1,003 | 612 |

Sum Popcorn

Add. Mark an X on the sum if the number is even.

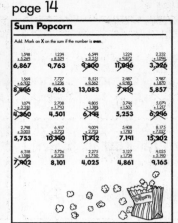

| 1,598 +5,249 | 1,234 +8,529 | 6,548 +3,251 | 1,224 +9,872 | 2,232 +1,094 |
| 6,867 | 9,763 | 9,800 | 11,096 | 3,326 |

| 1,564 +6,532 | 7,727 +1,236 | 8,521 +4,562 | 2,487 +4,983 | 3,987 +1,870 |
| 8,466 | 8,963 | 13,083 | 7,410 | 5,857 |

| 1,079 +3,281 | 2,708 +1,793 | 4,805 +1,385 | 3,746 +1,507 | 5,074 +1,212 |
| 4,360 | 4,501 | 6,190 | 5,253 | 6,296 |

| 2,748 +3,005 | 6,417 +3,723 | 9,009 +2,713 | 5,408 +1,783 | 8,175 +7,027 |
| 5,753 | 10,140 | 11,722 | 7,191 | 15,202 |

| 6,318 +1,584 | 5,726 +2,375 | 2,275 +1,750 | 3,127 +1,734 | 4,025 +5,140 |
| 7,902 | 8,101 | 4,025 | 4,861 | 9,165 |

Falling Amounts

Subtract.

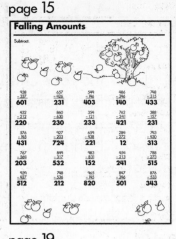

| 938 -337 | 657 -426 | 549 -346 | 486 -346 | 748 -315 |
| 601 | 231 | 403 | 140 | 433 |

| 432 -212 | 860 -630 | 354 -121 | 762 -341 | 388 -157 |
| 220 | 230 | 233 | 421 | 231 |

| 576 -145 | 927 -203 | 659 -438 | 284 -272 | 743 -430 |
| 431 | 724 | 221 | 12 | 313 |

| 767 -564 | 849 -317 | 983 -831 | 454 -213 | 788 -273 |
| 203 | 532 | 152 | 241 | 515 |

| 939 -427 | 748 -536 | 965 -145 | 847 -346 | 876 -533 |
| 512 | 212 | 820 | 501 | 343 |

Gardening Troubles

Why was the farmer looking for his keys in the garden?

Solve the problems. Then write the letters below to answer the riddle.

| T 29 | Y 36 | 65 | 93 | 71 |
| | 27 | 17 | 85 | 6 |

| 97 | 75 | 61 |
| T 38 | D 46 | H 67 | N 8 | E 48 |

| 68 | 46 | 56 | 71 |
| O 29 | U 28 | R 14 | 48 | 50 |

| 32 | 41 | 40 | 55 |
| W 16 | H 25 | P 12 | N 13 |

| 74 | 55 |
| W 49 | G 19 |

HE WAS HOPING THEYD
67 48 24 29 12 6 8 19 29 17 48 9 46

TURNIP
38 28 14 13 56 12

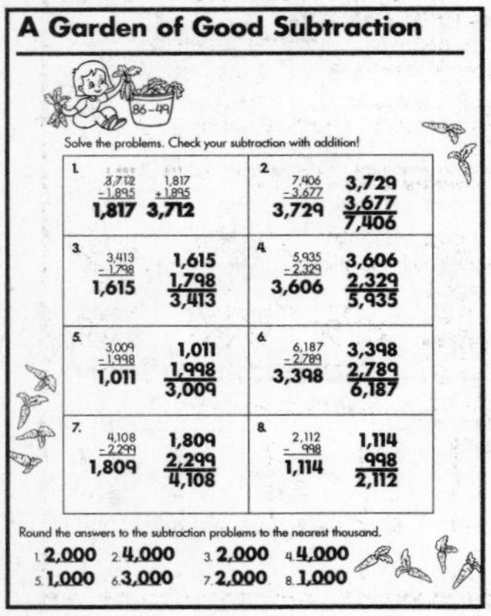

A Garden of Good Subtraction

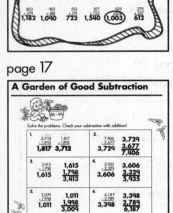

Solve the problems. Check your subtraction with addition!

| 1. 3,712 -1,895 | 1,817 1,817 1,817 3,712 | | 2. 7,406 -3,677 | 3,729 3,729 3,677 7,406 |
| 1,817 | 3,712 | | 3,729 | |

| 3. 3,413 -1,798 | 1,615 1,615 1,798 3,413 | 4. 5,935 -2,329 | 3,606 3,606 2,329 5,935 |
| 1,615 | | 3,606 | |

| 5. 3,009 -1,998 | 1,011 1,011 1,998 3,009 | 6. 6,187 -2,789 | 3,398 3,398 2,789 6,187 |
| 1,011 | | 3,398 | |

| 7. 4,108 -2,299 | 1,809 1,809 2,299 4,108 | 8. 2,112 -998 | 1,114 1,114 998 2,112 |
| 1,809 | | 1,114 | |

Round the answers to the subtraction problems to the nearest thousand.

1. 2,000 2. 4,000 3. 2,000 4. 4,000
5. 1,000 6. 3,000 7. 2,000 8. 1,000

Shopping Success

Add. Don't forget to line up your decimals!

| $748.78 +99.99 | $16.75 +23.89 | $215.84 +347.23 | $107.50 +341.98 |
| $165.77 | $40.64 | $563.12 | $449.48 |

| $403.28 +$174.72 | $304.78 +483.45 | $706.25 +38.43 | $700.99 +199.44 |
| $578.50 | $787.23 | $744.68 | $900.63 |

| $9,983.50 +2,560.91 | $2,283.25 +603.45 | $7,173.11 +3,840.88 | $3,186.65 |
| $12,524.41 | $2,886.90 | $11,013.99 | $15,203.12 |

After you've solved the problems, do the following. (Round to the nearest thousand.)

1. Circle the sums that can be rounded between $1,000 and $5,000.
2. Mark an X on the sums that can be rounded between $6,000 and $10,000.
3. Draw a box around the sums that can be rounded between $11,000 and $15,000.

18 Adding decimals; rounding numbers to thousands

Fruitful Fun with Decimals

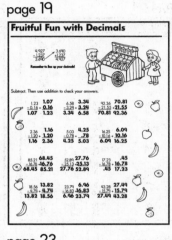

| 4.927 -1.237 | 3.690 +1.237 |
| 3.690 | 4.927 |

Remember to line up your decimals!

Subtract. Then use addition to check your answers.

| 1.23 -0.16 | 1.07 +0.16 | 6.58 -3.24 | 3.34 +3.24 | 92.36 -21.55 | 70.81 +21.55 |
| 1.07 | 1.23 | 3.34 | 6.58 | 70.81 | 92.36 |

| 2.36 -1.20 | 1.16 +1.20 | 5.03 -0.78 | 4.25 +0.78 | 16.25 -10.16 | 6.09 +10.16 |
| 1.16 | 2.36 | 4.25 | 5.03 | 6.09 | 16.25 |

| 85.21 -16.76 | 68.45 +16.76 | 52.89 -25.13 | 27.76 +25.13 | 17.23 -16.78 | .45 +16.78 |
| 68.45 | 85.21 | 27.76 | 52.89 | .45 | 17.23 |

| 18.56 -4.74 | 13.82 +4.74 | 23.79 -16.83 | 6.96 +16.83 | 27.49 -15.79 | 43.28 +15.79 |
| 13.82 | 18.56 | 6.96 | 23.79 | 27.49 | 43.28 |

Story Problems...Downloading

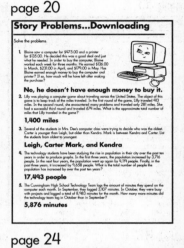

Solve the problems.

1. Blaine saw a computer for $1475.00 and a printer for $135.00. He decided this was a good deal and just what he needed. In order to buy the computer, Blaine worked each week for three months. He earned $136.00 in March, $231.00 in April, and $179.00 in May. Has Blaine earned enough money to buy the computer and printer? If so, how much will he have left after making the purchase?

No, he doesn't have enough money to buy it.

2. Lilly was playing a computer game about traveling across the United States. The object of this game is to keep track of the miles traveled. In the first round of the game, Lilly traveled 483 miles. In the second round, she encountered many problems and traveled only 281 miles. She had a successful third round and traveled 674 miles. What is the approximate total number of miles that Lilly traveled in the game?

1,400 miles

3. Several of the students in Mrs. Dee's computer class were trying to decide who was the oldest. Carter is younger than Leigh, but older than Kendra. Mark is between Kendra and Carter. List the students from oldest to youngest.

Leigh, Carter, Mark, and Kendra

4. The technology students have been studying the rise in population in their city over the past ten years in order to produce graphs. In the first three years, the population increased by 3,716 people. In the next four years, the population went up again by 4,191 people. Finally, in the past three years, it increased by 9,658 people. What is the total number of people the population has increased by over the past ten years?

17,493 people

5. The Cunningham High School Technology Team logs the amount of minutes they spend on the computer each month. In September, they logged 2,107 minutes. In October, they were busy with projects and logged a total of 8,983 minutes for the month. How many more minutes did the technology team log in October than in September?

5,876 minutes

Multiplication Madness

Complete the multiplication table. Do you see the pattern?

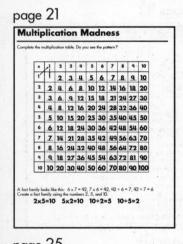

x	1	2	3	4	5	6	7	8	9
1	1	2	3	4	5	6	7	8	9
2	2	4	6	8	10	12	14	16	18	20
3	3	6	9	12	15	18	21	24	27	30
4	4	8	12	16	20	24	28	32	36	40
5	5	10	15	20	25	30	35	40	45	50
6	6	12	18	24	30	36	42	48	54	60
7	7	14	21	28	35	42	49	56	63	70
8	8	16	24	32	40	48	56	64	72	80
9	9	18	27	36	45	54	63	72	81	90
10	10	20	30	40	50	60	70	80	90	100

A fact family looks like this: 6 x 7 = 42, 7 x 6 = 42, 42 ÷ 6 = 7, 42 ÷ 7 = 6
Create a fact family using the numbers 2, 5, and 10.

2x5=10 5x2=10 10÷2=5 10÷5=2

Speeding Along

Solve the problems as fast as you can. Time yourself or ask someone to time you.

8 x3 24	7 x9 63	5 x3 15	8 x7 56	3 x9 27	6 x5 30	9 x1 9
6 x2 12	4 x9 36	9 x8 72	6 x4 24	4 x9 36	7 x5 35	4 x5 20
5 x9 45	8 x8 64	6 x7 42	9 x7 63	6 x4 24	1 x4 4	3 x2 6
1 x3 3	0 x9 0	6 x8 48	3 x7 21	2 x8 16	9 x1 9	3 x7 21
9 x9 81	4 x5 20	3 x9 27	2 x7 14	1 x8 8	5 x8 40	2 x8 16
7 x7 49	2 x9 18	0 x4 0	1 x0 0	8 x4 32	0 x5 0	8 x0 0
9 x7 63	5 x2 10	9 x2 18	8 x9 72	4 x3 12	2 x7 14	9 x3 27

Time: _____ Missed _____ out of 49

A Fresh Batch of Multiplication

Step 1: 24 x4 Multiply the ones place first. 4 x 4 = 16. Write the 6 in the ones place. Where do you remember 1?

Step 2: 24 x4 96 Now, multiply the tens place. 2 tens x 4 = 8 tens. Add the 1 ten to make it 9 tens.

Multiply.

96	207	114	42	204	60
165	172	58	180	85	280
54	78	224	84	378	130
75	136	54	64	154	132

Moving Along with Multiplication

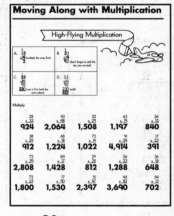

High-Flying Multiplication

Multiply.

924	2,064	1,508	1,197	840
912	1,224	1,022	4,914	391
2,808	1,428	812	1,288	648
1,800	1,530	2,397	3,690	702

Fast Forward with Multiplication

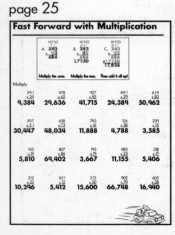

Multiply.

341 x29 9,384	478 x62 29,636	927 x45 41,715	841 x29 24,389	614 x83 50,962
547 x51 30,447	658 x73 48,034	743 x16 11,888	126 x38 4,788	239 x15 3,585
415 x14 5,810	807 x86 69,402	367 x19 6,967	485 x23 11,155	318 x17 5,406
312 x33 10,296	451 x12 5,412	312 x50 15,600	902 x74 66,748	605 x28 16,940

And They're Off

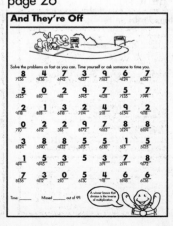

Solve the problems as fast as you can. Time yourself or ask someone to time you.

8 7)56	4 8)32	4 9)36	9 7)63	6 4)24	7 8)56
5 5)25	0 3)0	2 9)18	7 7)49	5 7)35	7 9)63
2 4)8	1 3)3	2 9)18	4 6)24	9 8)72	2 7)14
0 7)0	2 3)6	7 9)63	2 6)12	4 6)24	8 8)64
1 4)4	5 7)35	1 4)4	3 7)21	7 4)28	9 7)63
8 5)40	2 3)6	3 4)12	0 5)0	4 9)36	6 6)36

Time: _____ Missed _____ out of 49

Leaping Lizards Long Division

Divide to find the quotient. Watch out for remainders!

7 4)28	4 5)20	9r3 6)57	5r7 8)47	6r8 9)62	7r2 6)44
7 3)21	8r5 6)53	7r2 3)23	6 8)48	2 8)16	7r2 6)44
9r7 8)79	9r1 8)73	5 7)35	7r4 5)39	5 2)10	8 8)64
8 2)16	9r6 7)69	6 3)18	8r3 5)43	3 9)27	9 4)36

Dog Gone Division

Divide.

131 5)655	72 2)144	91 4)364	40 6)240	65 7)455
28 8)224	47 5)235	61 2)122	80 7)560	92 6)552
31 9)279	52 6)312	63 3)189	107 4)428	251 3)753
85 5)425	76 6)456	18 7)126	82 8)656	126 5)630

62 Answers

Take the Challenge!

Divide.
217 r... 547r2 644r2 925r2 951r5
581r1 315 1,393 323 837r1
368r1 312 534r3 431r1 891r1

Think About It

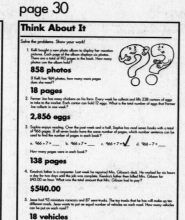

Solve the problems. Show your work!

1. Kelli bought a new photo album to display her vacation pictures. Each page of the album displays six photos. There are a total of 143 pages in the book. How many photos can the album hold?

858 photos

If Kelli has 964 photos, how many more pages does she need?

18 pages

2. Farmer Joe has many chickens on his farm. Every week he collects and fills 238 cartons of eggs to take to the market. Each carton can hold 12 eggs. What is the total number of eggs that Farmer Joe collects in one week?

2,856 eggs

3. Sophie enjoys reading. Over the past week and a half, Sophie has read seven books with a total of 966 pages. If all seven books have the same number of pages, which number sentence can be used to find the number of pages in each book?

a. 966 ÷ 7 = ___ b. 966 ÷ 7 = ___ c. 966 ÷ 7 ✓ d. 966 ÷ 7 = ___

How many pages were in each book?

138 pages

4. Kendra's father is a carpenter. Last week he repaired Mrs. Gibson's deck. He worked for six hours a day for two days until the job was complete. Kendra's father then billed Mrs. Gibson for $45.00 an hour. What was the total amount that Mrs. Gibson had to pay?

$540.00

5. Jesse had 93 miniature racecars and 87 semi-trucks. The toy tracks that he has will make up ten different roads. Jesse wants to put an equal number of vehicles on each road. How many vehicles can he put on each road?

18 vehicles

Delicious Fractions

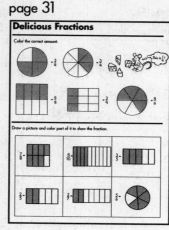

Color the correct amount.

Draw a picture and color part of it to show the fraction.

Fraction Double Take

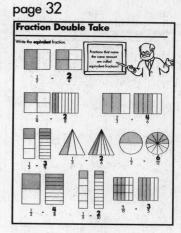

Write the equivalent fraction.

Fractions that name the same amount are called equivalent fractions.

Fraction Review I

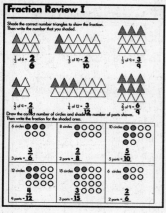

Shade the correct number triangles to show the fraction. Then write the number that you shaded.

Draw the correct number of circles and shade the number of parts shown. Then write the fraction for the shaded area.

Adding it Up

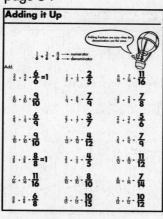

Adding fractions are easy when the denominators are the same.

$\frac{1}{6} + \frac{3}{6} = \frac{4}{6}$ ← numerator / ← denominator

Add.

Fraction Review II

Solve the fraction problems. Remember to watch your signs.

Fun with Fractions

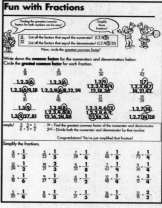

Finding the greatest common factors for both numbers can be easy!

Simplify the fractions.

Different, but the SAME!

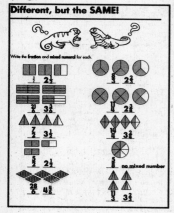

Write the fraction and mixed numeral for each.

That's Top Heavy

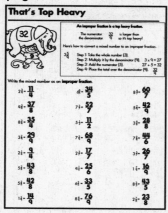

An improper fraction is a top heavy fraction.

The numerator $\frac{32}{9}$ is larger than the denominator so it's top heavy!

Here's how to convert a mixed number to an improper fraction.

$3\frac{5}{9}$ Step 1: Take the whole number (3).
Step 2: Multiply it by the denominator (9). 3 x 9 = 27
Step 3: Add the numerator (5). 27 + 5 = 32
Step 4: Place the total over the denominator (9).

Write the mixed number as an improper fraction.

What's the Value?

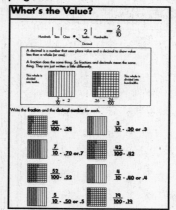

$\frac{2}{10} = \frac{2}{10}$

A decimal is a number that uses place value and a decimal to show value less than a whole (or one).

A fraction does the same thing. So fractions and decimals mean the same thing. They are just written a little differently.

Write the fraction and the decimal number for each.

Changing Units

The Golden Rule
When you change larger units to smaller units, you multiply.
When you change smaller units to larger units, you divide.

Convert each unit of measure.

If fencing is $2.00 per foot, how much would it cost to fence a dog run with a 36-yard perimeter for Brutus to have fun in?

36x3=108 feet 108x2=$216.00

The Rule of Thumb

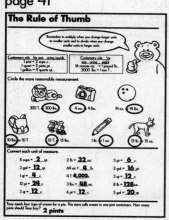

Remember to multiply when you change larger to smaller units or divide when you divide smaller units to larger units.

Circle the more reasonable measurement.

Convert each unit of measure.

Tony needs four cups of cream for a pie. The store sells cream in one-pint containers. How many pints should Tony buy? **2 pints**

Where in the World

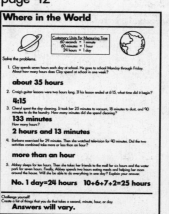

Customary Units For Measuring Time
60 seconds = 1 minute
60 minutes = 1 hour
24 hours = 1 day

Solve the problems.

1. Clay spends seven hours each day at school. He goes to school Monday through Friday. About how many hours does Clay spend at school in one week?

about 35 hours

2. Craig's guitar lessons were two hours long. If his lesson ended at 6:15, what time did it begin?

4:15

3. Cheryl spent the day cleaning. It took her 25 minutes to vacuum, 18 minutes to dust, and 90 minutes to do the laundry. How many minutes did she spend cleaning?

133 minutes

2 hours and 13 minutes

4. Barbara exercised for 24 minutes. Then she watched television for 40 minutes. Did the two activities combined take more or less than an hour?

more than an hour

5. Abbey sleeps for ten hours. Then she takes her friends to the mall for six hours and the water park for seven hours. Finally, Abbey spends two hours eating meals and helping her mom around the house. Will she be able to do this in one day? Explain your answer.

No. 1 day=24 hours 10+6+7+2=25 hours

Challenge yourself!
Create a list of things that you do that takes a second, minute, hour, or day.

Answers will vary.

Elapsed Time

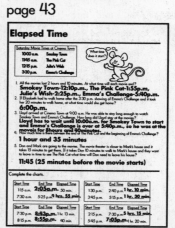

Saturday Movie Times at Cinema Town
10:00 a.m. Smokey Town
11:45 a.m. The Pink Cat
12:15 p.m. Julie's Wish
3:30 p.m. Emma's Challenge

1. All the movies last 2 hours and 10 minutes. At what time will each movie end?
Smokey Town-12:10p.m., The Pink Cat-1:55p.m., Julie's Wish-2:25p.m., Emma's Challenge-5:40p.m.

2. If Elizabeth had to walk home after the 3:30 p.m. showing of Emma's Challenge and it took her 20 minutes to walk home, at what time would she get home?
6:00p.m.

3. Lloyd arrived at Cinema Town at 9:00 a.m. He was able to stay long enough to watch Smokey Town and Emma's Challenge. How long did Lloyd stay at the movie?
Lloyd had to wait until 10:00a.m. for Smokey Town to start and Emma's Challenge is over at 5:40p.m., so he was at the movies for 8hours and 90minutes.

4. How many hours?
1 hour and 35 minutes

5. Dan and Mark are going to the movies. The movie theater is closer to Mark's house and it takes 15 minutes to get there. If it takes Dan 10 minutes to walk to Mark's house and they want to leave in time to see The Pink Cat-what time will Don need to leave his house?
11:45 (25 minutes before the movie starts)

Complete the charts.

Start Time	End Time	Elapsed Time
1:15 a.m.	2:05 a.m.	50 min.
7:30 a.m.	5:25 p.m.	9 hrs. 55 min.

Start Time	End Time	Elapsed Time
1:30 p.m.	2:40 p.m.	1 hr. 10 min.
3:45 p.m.		1 hr. 30 min.

Start Time	End Time	Elapsed Time
7:30 a.m.	8:43a.m.	1 hr. 13 min.
8:15 p.m.	8:55 p.m.	40 min.

Start Time	End Time	Elapsed Time
2:15 p.m.		5 hrs. 15 min.
5:45 p.m.	7:05 p.m.	1 hr. 20 min.

Perimeter, It's What's Around You!

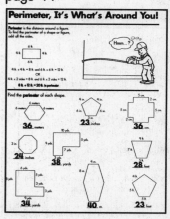

Perimeter is the distance around a figure.
To find the perimeter of a shape or figure, add all the sides.

Find the perimeter of each shape.

36 meters **23** inches **36** feet
24 inches **38** yards **28** feet
34 yards **40** m. **23** feet

Awesome Amounts of Area

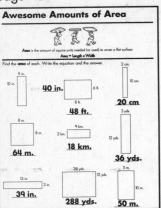

Area is the amount of square units needed (or used) to cover a flat surface.

Area = Length x Width

Find the **area** of each. Write the equation and the answer.

40 in.
20 cm
48 ft.
64 m.
18 km.
36 yds.
39 in.
288 yds.
50 m.

Amazing Angles

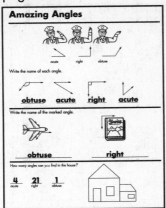

acute   right   obtuse

Write the name of each angle.

obtuse   acute   right   acute

Write the name of the marked angle.

obtuse   right

How many angles can you find in the house?

4 acute   **21** right   **1** obtuse

Measuring Around

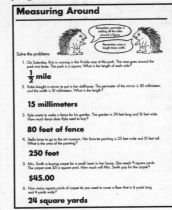

Solve the problems.

1. On Saturday, Kris is running in the 4-mile race at the park. The race goes around the park two times. The park is a square. What is the length of each side?

½ mile

2. Katie bought a mirror to put in her dollhouse. The perimeter of the mirror is 50 millimeters and the width is 10 millimeters. What is the length?

15 millimeters

3. Kyle wants to make a fence for his garden. The garden is 24 feet long and 16 feet wide. How much fence does Kyle need to buy?

80 feet of fence

4. Stella loves to go to the art museum. Her favorite painting is 25 feet wide and 10 feet tall. What is the area of the painting?

250 feet

5. Mrs. Smith is buying carpet for a small room in her house. She needs 9 square yards. The carpet costs $5 a square yard. How much will Mrs. Smith pay for the carpet?

$45.00

6. How many square yards of carpet do you need to cover a floor that is 6 yards long and 4 yards wide?

24 square yards

Rounding Numbers

Round the numbers to the nearest ten.

248 **250**   63 **60**   71 **70**   326 **330**   104 **100**

97 **100**   56 **60**   1,254 **1,250**   83 **80**   653 **650**

45 **50**   132 **130**   87 **90**   49 **50**   99 **100**

354 **350**   16 **20**   308 **310**   757 **760**   37 **40**

Round the numbers to the nearest hundred.

3,743 **3,700**   12,278 **12,300**   374 **400**   145 **100**

546 **500**   2,453 **2,500**   98 **100**   4,389 **4,400**

2,614 **2,600**   194 **200**   7,642 **7,600**   893 **900**

216 **200**   703 **700**   1,783 **1,800**   574 **600**

Round the numbers to the nearest thousand.

17,524 **18,000**   6,426 **6,000**   3,941 **4,000**   2,642 **3,000**

4,834 **5,000**   4,216 **4,000**   1,823 **2,000**   9,487 **9,000**

23,573 **24,000**   6,840 **7,000**   7,927 **8,000**   1,431 **1,000**

16,763 **17,000**   5,327 **5,000**   9,849 **10,000**   3,347 **3,000**

Addition Review

Add.

289	**895**	**93**	**1,290**	**2,143**
369	**791**	**6,495**	**1,526**	**90**
790	**147**	**5,008**	**865**	**652**
99	**1,036**	**9,058**	**490**	**4,024**
635	**3,492**	**79**	**7,111**	**4,176**

Multiplication Review I

Multiply.

63	**56**	**30**	**12**	**40**	**42**
28	**36**	**35**	**18**	**36**	**24**
49	**21**	**45**	**64**	**30**	**63**
36	**81**	**25**	**32**	**42**	**12**
54	**40**	**20**	**63**	**56**	**72**
24	**48**	**27**	**28**	**45**	**15**

Multiplication Review II

Multiply.

468	**161**	**1,924**	**196**	**544**	**133**
664	**7,452**	**632**	**912**	**340**	**765**
1,083	**189**	**2,294**	**402**	**322**	**216**
133	**1,869**	**195**	**2,496**	**497**	**1,162**
1,404	**108**	**1,102**	**141**	**676**	**117**
328	**1,206**	**237**	**1,577**	**465**	**684**

Multiplication Review III

Remember: Multiply the ones place first. Multiply the tens place second. Then add them together!

25,746	**7,803**	**28,861**	**6,646**	**10,824**
57,305	**6,592**	**35,244**	**6,165**	**6,061**
58,688	**37,352**	**21,717**	**19,170**	**8,496**
60,236	**25,928**	**3,003**	**6,960**	**10,121**
73,305	**27,846**	**39,216**	**3,276**	**6,528**

Division Review I

Divide.

2	**2**	**8**	**0**	**5**	**5**
9	**9**	**7**	**2**	**1**	**5**
7	**7**	**10**	**2**	**9**	**9**
9	**7**	**5**	**6**	**0**	**9**
6	**4**	**7**	**7**	**2**	**5**
6	**2**	**1**	**0**	**7**	**10**
4	**7**	**8**	**7**	**0**	**7**

Division Review II

Divide.

13	**14**	**24r1**	**15**	**41**	**26**
24	**17**	**13**	**36**	**14**	**12**
15r3	**13r6**	**12**	**27**	**24r2**	**11r5**
49	**19**	**19**	**18r2**	**13**	**12**
44	**23**	**13r5**	**23r2**	**19r4**	

Division Review III

Divide.

91r1	**62r3**	**82r1**	**90r7**	**157r1**
39r3	**116**	**63r3**	**41**	**74r5**
290	**84r4**	**107**	**194r3**	**43**
183	**141r3**	**52r1**	**131**	**124r4**

Let Your Brilliance Shine!

1. Write the numbers using Roman Numerals.
66 **LXVI**   47 **XLVII**

2. 4,743 **5,142**   3,482 **2,748**

3. (4 x 7) - 4 ___ 8 = (6 x 5)
  ○ a. >   ● b. <
  ○ c. =   ○ d. ≠

4. Round the numbers to the nearest thousand.
7,000   3,000   2,000

5. 4,609.72 - 526.96 =
  ○ a. 4,082.73   ● b. 4,083.76
  ○ c. 4,082.78   ○ d. 4,183.78

6. 84 ÷ 9 =
  ○ a. 8.50   ○ b. 92 r3
  ● c. 9 r3   ○ d. 4 r3

7. Write the standard form of three million, forty six thousand, eight hundred three.
3,046,803

8. Write the word form for 5,870,403.
five million, eight hundred seventy thousand, four hundred three

9. Todd's four friends have no sports trading cards of their own. Todd has 246 baseball cards and 134 football cards. He would like to share his cards with his friends. How many cards will Todd and each of his friends receive? Will they all receive the same amount?
76 cards each
Yes, they will all receive the same amount.

10. Priscilla and her three friends like to play with dolls at her house. She has quite a collection and always likes to share evenly. Priscilla has 76 dolls. She wants each person to have the same number of dolls. How many will each person get? Will there be any dolls left over?
19 dolls each
No, there will not be any dolls left over.

11. Kyle feeds his dog Skippy twice a day. Skippy eats a cup of food each time he is fed. How many cups of food will Skippy eat in a four-week period?
7x4=28 days   28x2 cups=56 cups

Show What You Know!

1. Find the missing number in this pattern.
176, 171, 156
  ○ a. 169
  ○ b. 166
  ○ c. 170
  ● d. 165

2. 187 **17,204**   904 **68,704**

3. I am n 634.
I am even.
My digits total 17.
What number am I?
  ○ a. 699   ○ c. 736   ○ d. 566
  ● b. 674

4. Round the numbers to the nearest hundred.
3,700   8,300   7,600

5. 132.78 + 8,746.23 = **8,879.01**

6. 11,756 ÷ 9 = **1,219 r4**

7. Write the expanded form of 8,746.
8,000 + 700 + 40 + 6

8. 4 hundreds + 11 tens + 7 ones = ___
  ○ a. 417   ○ c. 418
  ● b. 517   ○ d. 507

9. Jill had saved her babysitting money for several months. She has a total of $89.75 and is going to buy a portable CD player for $37.95 and a CD for 15.99. How much money will Jill have left?
$35.81

10. Chad sells newspapers. He delivered 378 papers on Monday, 264 papers on Tuesday, and 418 papers on Wednesday. About how many papers did Chad delivered so far this week?
about 1,100

11. Laney was cleaning her family's closets and found they had a total of 31 pairs of shoes. After talking with the girls at school, she found that Christina's family has 47 pairs of shoes and Emily's small family has 26 pairs of shoes. What method could be used to find how many more pairs of shoes Christina's family has than Emily's family?
  ○ a. Subtract 31 from 47.
  ○ b. Add 26 and 31.
  ○ c. Add 26 and 31 and subtract from 47.
  ● d. Subtract 26 from 47.

Fractions and Decimals

Numbers less than a whole can be written two ways—as a fraction or as a decimal. Rewrite the numbers as fractions or decimals.

2/10 = **.2**   40/100 = **.40**   8/10 = **.8**

53/100 = **.53**   46 = **46/100**   79/100 = **.79**

56/100 = **.56**   31 = **.31**   5/10 = **.5**

2/10 = **.2**   28 = **.28**   1/10 = **.1**

83/100 = **.83**   98 = **.98**   4/10 = **.4**

62/100 = **.62**   92 = **.92**   43/100 = **.43**

37/100 = **.37**   18 = **.18**

51/100 = **.51**   27 = **.27**   82/100 = **.82**

3/10 = **.3**   8/10 = **.8**   19/10 = **.19**

21 = **.21**   79 = **.79**   13/10 = **.13**

63/100 = **.63**   43 = **43/100**   74/100 = **.74**

Mixed Review I

1. Which is the most likely to have the capacity of 2 gallons?
  ○ a. kitchen sink
  ○ b. water jug
  ● c. bath tub
  ○ d. soda can

2. A bathtub would have the capacity of:
  ○ a. 3 gallons   ○ b. 4 pint
  ● c. 50 liters   ○ d. 1 cup

3. Grandma was in the baking mood. She decided to make a cake for each of her five grandchildren. Each cake called for eight ounces of cocoa. How many ounces of cocoa did grandma have to buy?
40 ounces

4. Bill needs his morning coffee. If his coffee pot holds nine cups of coffee and he pours himself one cup. How much is in the pot now?
3 cups

5. An elephant would be measured in what?
  ○ a. pounds   ○ b. tons
  ○ c. millimeters   ○ d. meters

6. An encyclopedia would be weighed in what?
  ○ a. grams   ● b. kilograms
If one encyclopedia weighed 2 ___ **kg**
how much would 8 weigh? **16 kg**

7. Tina has a bag of marbles that weighs 18 grams. If Jeff's bag of marbles weighs 27 grams, how much more does Jeff's bag weigh than Tina's?
9 grams

8. A new baby weighs 7 lbs., how many ounces is that?
112 ounces

9. Lacey and Tim competed in a dance marathon. They danced for a total of 4 hours and 28 minutes. How many minutes did Lacey and Tim dance?
  ○ a. 240 min.   ○ b. 258 min.
  ○ c. 158 min.   ● d. 268 min.
2 hours and 45 minutes

Mixed Review II

Solve the problems.

1. Round 564 to the nearest ten.
  ○ a. 570   ● b. 565   ○ c. 560   ○ d. 600

2. Round 5,758 to the nearest hundred.
  ○ a. 6,000   ○ b. 5,800   ● c. 5,760   ○ d. 5,700

3. Akira bought eight hair ribbons. Each ribbon was 18 inches long. How many yards of ribbon did Akira purchase?
  ○ a. 8 yds. 7 in.   ○ b. 4 yds.
  ● c. 1 yd. 10 in.   ○ d. 4 yds. 2 in.

4. The circus ran out of peanuts and nickels to make change so it had to round everything to the nearest $0.10. What will a $0.78 item cost?
  ○ a. $0.70   ● b. $0.80
  ○ c. $1.00   ○ d. $0.70

5. 578 693 **15,606** **33,264**

6. 278 ÷ 4 = **69r2**   3,764 ÷ 8 = **470r4**

7. How much of the pizza has been eaten? Simplify your fraction.
2/8 = 1/4

8. Karen is older than David. Mark is older than Karen. Angie is older than Mark. Who is the oldest?
Angie

9. Connie has a doctor's appointment at 3:30 p.m. She was held up at school and then home until 4:50 p.m. How late was Connie?
1 hour and 20 minutes

10. Find the greatest common factor for each fraction and simplify.
2/8 = 1/4   **2/12 = 1/6**   **10/16 = 5/8**